Praying the Daily Gospels

Other Works by the Author

A Season for Change:
Praying the Gospels of Lent

◆

Handbook for Spiritual Growth:
A Guide for Catholics

◆

Twelve Steps to Spiritual Wholeness:
A Christian Pathway

◆

Freedom From Codependency

◆

Lessons in Loving:
Developing Relationship Skills

◆

Pathways to Serenity

Becoming a New Person:
Twelve Steps to Christian Growth

Catholic Answers to Fundamentalists' Questions

———————

Coauthored with Lisa Bellecci-st.romain
Living Together, Loving Together
A Spiritiual Guide to Marriage

Praying the Daily Gospels

A Guide to Meditation

Philip St. Romain

LIGUORI
PUBLICATIONS

One Liguori Drive
Liguori, MO 63057-9999
(314) 464-2500

ISBN 0-89243-841-X
Library of Congress Catalog Card Number: 95-76472

Originally published by Ave Marie Press © 1984

Contents

The Season of Lent

The Season of Easter

Ordinary Time After Pentecost

Preface

The first edition of *Praying the Daily Gospels* was written in 1982. I had been meditating for several years on the gospel readings used in the daily liturgy of the Church, and I had journals filled with reflections to help me formulate the meditations and questions contained in the book. I initially wrote these down in cursive and later typed them up as my "hard copy," eventually sending the completed manuscript to Frank Cunningham at Ave Maria Press. I knew no one with a personal computer or word processor. This was simply the way things were done by most writers.

Writing today has become much easier, thanks to the many extraordinary developments in computer technology. Yet when it comes to prayer, we are not helped much by all these advances. We still must slow down, quiet our minds, and open ourselves to the presence of God mediated through the sacred word. That is what *Praying the Daily Gospels* has helped more than thirty thousand Christians do since its first printing in 1984.

The questions I have been asked most about the earlier edition have been: "What about the different cycles; do you have the gospel readings for each year?" "What about the first reading for each day?" "What about the Sunday gospels? Do you include them too?" Surely these will be asked about the present edition also.

To respond briefly: the same gospel passages are used each year in the two-year cycle for the daily liturgies, although a different gospel is used for special feast days. The first readings for weekday liturgies follow a two-year cycle, and the Sunday readings follow a three-year cycle. A meditation guide that includes all the feast days, the first readings, and the Sunday readings would comprise several volumes and be cumbersome and costly. My intention for this work, then as now, was simply to stimulate daily prayer based on the daily gospel readings of the Church's liturgical seasons, not to provide a meditation companion to the Lectionary. I hope this second edition will be helpful unto this end.

Praying the Daily Gospels was written during my years of association with the Catholic community at Louisiana State University in Baton Rouge. Father Dan Drinan, Sister Lydia Champagne, and Father John Edmonds were ministerial colleagues who helped critique the original manuscript. Christ the Servant Cenacle and St. George and St. Patrick Parishes helped pilot the Lenten section and offered valuable feedback concerning the content and organization. Frank Cunningham of Ave Maria Press provided encouragement and editorial assistance.

After the first edition had gone out of print, Father Tom Santa, president of Liguori Publications, expressed an interest in publishing a second edition through Liguori. He also encouraged the issuing of a Lenten guide based on this work (including the Sunday readings) entitled *A Season for Change* which was published by Liguori Publications in 1994. I am indebted to him for these and many other forms of support. Liguori editor, Barbara McElroy, has contributed to making improvements in this second edition.

No married man with three children can find the time to write and think without the support of an extremely understanding wife. Thanks, Lisa! You helped make this possible.

PHILIP ST. ROMAIN
JANUARY 1995

Introduction

Prayer is a hunger experienced by millions of people today. Numerous faith renewal movements sweeping through the Church in recent years have deepened in many people an awareness of Jesus Christ as personal lord and savior. People are discovering anew a love for the Word of God in Scripture, striving enthusiastically to understand what is there and to prayerfully reflect on what it calls them to become.

Learning to pray with Scripture does not come easily, however. Always there are the distractions we bring to prayer, in addition to the constant struggle to find a quiet time to be alone with God. Once settled, we face the task of identifying a Scripture to reflect upon—not always as easy as it might sound. I, and many others, have used a variety of approaches when praying with Scripture.

I have gone through periods when I moved systematically through a section of the Bible, selecting a few verses as food for meditation for each prayer session. This worked well, except for the days when I wound up with a genealogy or a salutation or something else that didn't seem to help me lift my mind and heart to God as I had hoped. Another approach involves "cracking" the Bible open, selecting a passage from one of the pages in view. This has proven to be a powerful experience at times, almost like confronting an oracle, but at other times it has produced the same kinds of dry materials that the systematic process did. (Bible cracking also evoked in me a kind of superstition about the word of God, as though there were something extraordinarily significant on the pages to which I had opened.) Neither approach provided lasting satisfaction.

The answer to my struggle to find Scriptures with which to pray came through several spiritual writers, most notably Henri Nouwen, who suggested using the Scripture passages for the Church's liturgy of the day. I began accepting the daily liturgical Scriptures for prayerful consideration as I would have from a director on a retreat; I soon discovered that the two passages provided more than I could digest in my few minutes of solitude. A choice therefore had to be made: Was I to pray with the first reading or with the gospel? I chose the gospel, of course, since in the gospels we encounter Jesus in a very special way. The gospels present us with the Church's faith-filled memories of the life and teachings of Jesus. That is what I needed to encounter in prayer.

Praying with the gospel passage from the liturgy of the day has been a rewarding experience for me during the past few years. I have found that this allowed for a fairly comprehensive covering of all four gospels in a year's time while deeply enriching my experience of the Mass on the days I attended. On days when I could not go to Mass, praying with the Church's selections gave me a sense of being more in tune with the rhythms and movements developed through the seasons of the liturgical year.

This has been a powerful experience for me and it is why I recommend it wholeheartedly.

It is important here to point out the difference between praying with Scripture and studying Scripture. The study of Scripture is an important complement to prayer, informing the mind concerning the contexts and meanings that both limit and illuminate the messages of Scripture. An overbalance of pious reflection can lead to a narrow perspective on Scripture; conversely, too much exegetical reflection can lead one to approach Scripture in an analytical frame of mind rather than in openness to encounter God. This balancing between piety and formal study of Scripture is a struggle that any committed Christian must not avoid, for the consequences of neglect either way can have detrimental influences on personal growth.

In the pages that follow I hope to stimulate prayer by focusing on the gospel passages for the Church's seasonal weekday liturgies. For each day, a short note concerning contextual and theological considerations is provided to help dispose the mind for reflection on the questions and ideas which follow. These reflection stimuli are intended to help the reader internalize the meaning of the gospels and apply its message to the concrete circumstances of life.

I have found that writing in a journal is helpful during prayer, and can provide material to refer to from time to time. With journal, Bible, and meditation guide, then, let us join the Church in her prayer journey through the year.

How to Pray
With Scripture

To make the most of this opportunity to grow in your relationship with God, I recommend that you set aside at least twenty minutes every day for prayer. For most people, first thing in the morning works best. That way, the fruit of their prayer nourishes them all day. If early morning is not possible, find another time that will work for you. And, of course, if you want to go beyond twenty minutes, that would be wonderful!

Having chosen your time, you should be faithful to the disciplines of solitude and silence. While there is a time and a place for communal prayer, this time is to be spent alone with God, to develop your own friendship with him so you will be able to share this with others in communal prayer. Try to find a place where it will be quiet. Get away from the phone, and turn off the television and radio. Tell your family that unless there is an emergency, you do not want to be disturbed.

For your time of silence and solitude with God, I recommend the following method of praying with Scripture:

1. **Quieting.** Take a few moments to settle in. Find a comfortable position, and ask the Holy Spirit to lead you in this time of prayer. Let your mind become calm by noticing your bodily sensations, the sound in the room around you, the rhythm and feel of your own breathing. Do not be disturbed if your mind does not become completely silent. It hardly ever will.

2. **Listening.** When you are ready, pick up the Bible and read the psalm for the day. This will help to direct your thoughts toward God. Pause briefly, and then read the short commentary on the gospel of the day. Now read the gospel slowly and prayerfully, as though it were a letter from God to you. If a particular word or phrase from the passage speaks to you, pause with it for a while, repeating this word or phrase in your mind or on your lips. Let its meaning penetrate you deeply.

3. **Prayer.** When you are ready, tell God in your own words what this word or passage means to you. It can be in the form of a feeling, a question, a petition, or maybe just loving silence. Continue reading the passage, pausing at meaningful words and phrases and responding in prayer until you have finished the reading, or until you are out of time.

4. **Reflection.** If time permits, or if you find few words or phrases that hold your attention for very long, consider the questions and suggestions for meditation. You might find it beneficial to record your responses in a journal or notebook.

5. **Resolution.** As a result of this time of quieting, listening, praying, and reflecting, what will you

strive to do (or not to do) today? A suggested resolution—in the form of a prayer for a particular grace—is provided for most days.

6. **Loving silence.** Conclude your prayer time by resting in the awareness of God's love for you. You do not need to say anything during this time. Just open your heart and your mind to God, and allow the fruit of your prayer to take root in your being. If you enjoy this experience of resting in God, extend your prayer time to allow it to deepen.

If, during prayer,
you do nothing
but bring your heart
from distraction
again and again
into God's presence,
though it went away
every time you
brought it back,
your time would be
very well employed.

SAINT FRANCIS DE SALES

The Season
of Advent

The season of Advent marks the beginning of the Church's liturgical year. During this season, preparation for the coming of the Messiah is stressed through Old Testament prophets and Jesus' fulfillment of the prophecies. We are invited through these readings to better prepare our own hearts for Christ's coming into our lives.

First Week in Advent

Monday
Psalm 122:1-9
Matthew 8:5-11
(Healing a centurion's servant)

Jesus brings health and wholeness to a Gentile. For the early Church, this incident was a reminder that the Messiah and the graces he won for us are to be extended to all people and not just to converts from Judaism. Jesus wants to come to everyone.

- Let your imagination re-create this gospel scene; put yourself in the place of the centurion. See Jesus walking along the road; watch as he notes your approach and gives you his full attention; note his response to your requests for healing in your life and in the lives of your loved ones.

- Make a list in your journal of the people in your life for whom you have been called to be an incarnation of God's grace. How can you be a better channel of grace to each of them?

Tuesday
Psalm 72:1,7-8,12-13,17
Luke 10:21-24
(Jesus rejoices)

Jesus had sent his seventy-two disciples out among the people to announce a forthcoming visitation. When the disciples returned to him they were overjoyed that the people were eager to see Jesus. Jesus' delight shows that the gospel is not meant to be a burdensome task.

- Share with God something that has recently happened in your life which you believe helped you and/or another to grow in some way. Let yourself imagine Jesus expressing delight over this.

- How do you feel about Jesus having come? Do you take the Incarnation for granted? What does the Incarnation mean to you?

Wednesday
Psalm 23:1-6
Matthew 15:29-37
(Jesus feeds the crowd)

In this passage and in others where miracles are discussed, it is not as important to focus on the extraordinary deed as on what it means. Bread and fish are symbols of the Eucharist; this passage emphasizes Jesus' power to nourish us in spirit, mind, and body.

- Jesus turned a small offering into a feast. What are some of the talents God has given you that you can offer toward the building of his kingdom? How can you better offer these gifts to God?

Thursday
Psalm 118:1,8-9,19-21,25-27
Matthew 7:21,24-27
(Build wisely)

We build our lives on certain beliefs and principles. Jesus tells us that life will test us in many ways and that if we have built our lives on foundations other than him, life will destroy us.

- In your journal, make a sketch of yourself; use a symbol of a house to represent yourself. What foundation is supporting this house? What kinds of forces are bearing down on your house at this time in your life, threatening to tear it down?

- Pray for the grace to build your life more firmly on Christ.

Friday
Psalm 27:1,4,13-14
Matthew 9:27-31
(Jesus cures two blind men)

Jesus was very aware that his actions and words were misinterpreted by those who had their own ideas about what the messiah should be. He did not fit the role of the political monarch some wanted, nor was he committed to the cause of Jewish nationalism. He saw himself more as a loving servant and sought frequently to deflect attention away from himself toward his Father.

- If you could ask and receive one gift from God, what would you choose? Hear Jesus ask you, "Are you confident I can do this for you?"

- Ask for the grace to strengthen your faith in God's providence.

Saturday
Psalm 147:1-6
Matthew 9:35-10:1,6-8
(Jesus shares his mission with us)

One of the overwhelming implications of the Incarnation is that God became human so that humans might become God. Co-creator with his father, Jesus nevertheless chooses to share with us his ministry of building the kingdom. We are co-creators and co-redeemers of the world with him and with the One who sent him.

- At the sight of human suffering, Jesus was moved to compassion. How do you usually feel when you are exposed to the reality of human suffering, whether in your own life or through the media?

- How do you feel about the statement, "The kingdom of heaven is at hand"? Do you believe it?

Second Week in Advent

Monday
Psalm 85:9-14
Luke 5:17-26
(Jesus heals a paralyzed man)

"Who but God alone can forgive sins?" mutter the scribes and the Pharisees in today's reading. Jesus replies by showing them that the same love which heals the body can also heal a guilt-ridden spirit.

- Do you love your body? Do you believe that your own bodily health is a value important to God? Why? Why not? Spend some time thanking God for your health, even if you do not enjoy perfect health.

- Hear Jesus saying, "As for you, your sins are forgiven." Pray for the grace to believe that you are a forgiven sinner.

Tuesday
Psalm 96:1-3,10-13
Matthew 18:12-14
(The Good Shepherd)

God loves individuals. This is a revelation sometimes hard for us to grasp—we think that God is too busy running the universe to love us. Yet Jesus tells us that God's greatest joy comes when an individual decides to break from sin and join his Father's fold.

- With whom do you identify most in today's parable: the stray sheep, the ninety-nine faithful ones, or the shepherd in search of the stray? Why?

- How do you usually feel when you hear others sharing their conversion experiences? Do you rejoice with them?

Wednesday
Psalm 103:1-4,8,10
Matthew 11:28-30
(The gentle Christ)

We sometimes hear people sharing their confusion and struggle as they try to discover what God's will is for them. Today's reading reminds us that God's will is meant to be refreshing, not burdensome. God is a loving support, not a judgmental taskmaster.

- What does Jesus mean when he says his yoke is easy, his burden light? How do you experience this?

- Spend some time with the words "Come to me." Let yourself feel God's desire for you to be with him.

Thursday
Psalm 145:1,9-13
Matthew 11:11-15
(Jesus praises John the Baptist)

The figure of John the Baptist is one revered by the Church. John was apparently one of the greatest of Jewish prophets, one believed by many to be the messiah. The Church has long considered John the forerunner of the Messiah, Jesus Christ. In today's reading Jesus himself identifies John as the spirit of Elijah who had been prophesied to usher in the new age.

- The spirit of John the Baptist was a spirit of bold-ness and courage which Winston Churchill main-tained made all other virtues possible. Are you courageous in standing up for the gospel?

- Pray for the grace to let go of fear in your life.

Friday
Psalm 1:1-6
Matthew 11:16-19
(The fickleness of the crowds)

It is impossible to please everybody, Jesus learns. Some consider Jesus too liberal in his following of the Law, and they condemn him. These critics are probably the same people who criticized John for being too strict. But Jesus does not cater to public opinion. He is intent only on doing the will of his Father.

- How do the opinions of others influence you? Do you find it easy to go against the crowd? When do you usually find this necessary?

- How do you feel about people who are noncon-formists for noble reasons? Why?

Saturday
Psalm 80:2-3,15-16,18-19
Matthew 17:10-13
(On John and Elijah)

The Old Testament prophets wrote a number of things concerning the origins and times of the Mes-siah. They expected that he would be of the house of David, born in Bethlehem, and be ushered in by the prophet Elijah who would "turn the hearts of the fathers toward their children, and the hearts of children toward their fathers" (Malachi 3:24). Jesus tells his disciples that John the Baptist has fulfilled Elijah's role.

- How do you invite the Messiah to work in your life? What virtues are you cultivating to prepare yourself for his work within you? Think of a person who plays an important role in your life but whom you have neglected recently. Make a resolution to let this person know how much you appreciate him or her.

Third Week in Advent

(If December 17 to 24 fall during this week, refer to Late Advent readings on pages 37 to 41.)

Monday
Psalm 25:4-9
Matthew 21:23-27
(The authority of Jesus)

The Jewish religious authorities tried many times to trap Jesus in some kind of philosophical dilemma. In today's reading, we find them baiting Jesus by asking him about the sources of his authority. Recognizing the trap, Jesus exposes their hypocrisy and political fears.

- When was the last time you felt attacked because of your religious beliefs? How did you respond?

- What does *authority* mean to you? How do you usually feel about authorities?

- Pray for the grace to be more submissive to the authority of Christ.

Tuesday
Psalm 34:2-3,6-7,17-19,23
Matthew 21:28-32
(The meaning of obedience)

Many people rebel against the idea of obedience because they believe it entails mindless submission. In today's parable, however, we learn that those who choose to obey the will of God by living a life of love are exercising human freedom in the best way.

- An old axiom says that the road to hell is paved with good intentions. Do you agree with this? Why? Why not?

- Is there something that needs to be done to make your life or your family's life richer but which you have procrastinated beginning? Resolve to make a start today.

Wednesday
Psalm 85:9-14
Luke 7:18-23
(John's disciples seek the Messiah)

It is apparent that even John the Baptist is surprised at the kind of Messiah Jesus is turning out to be. Jesus reassures his imprisoned friend that making people whole is more important than political glory.

- Do you often question who Jesus was and what he was about? Do you find such questioning a threat to your faith? Why? Why not?

- How do you feel about the response Jesus gave to John's disciples? How well does his response describe your own lifestyle?

Thursday
Psalm 30:2,4-6,11-13
Luke 7:24-30
(Jesus praises John)

Many people had gone out of their way to hear John the Baptist and to be baptized by him. Jesus affirms their recognition of John's greatness, but he challenges them to grow to even greater heights through the Spirit.

- How do you feel challenged by Christ to grow in the Spirit?

- Pray to become aware of your own giftedness. Spend some time thanking God for these gifts.

Friday
Psalm 67:2-3,5,7-8
John 5:33-36
(The testimony of Jesus and John)

John the Baptist, our Advent guide, was the one who prepared the people for the works that Jesus was to do among them. In today's reading Jesus points to these works as evidence that God has sent him.

- Look over the works you have performed during the past two days. To whom do they testify?

- What kinds of charitable works have you neglected lately? Make a resolution to begin at least one of them today.

Late Advent

December 17
Psalm 72:3-4,7-8,17
Matthew 1:1-17
(Matthew's genealogy)

Genealogies are among the most difficult Scriptures to use as grist for prayer. Matthew's carefully constructed genealogy traces Jesus' origins back through the line of David; the prophet Nathan had foreseen the Messiah would come from this royal family. Though the accuracy of this genealogy is contested by some Scripture scholars, it nevertheless emphasizes the human side of the Messiah.

- Make a diagram sketching your own family tree. Go back two or three generations if you can.

- Glancing over your family tree, try to recall at least one way in which each individual you've listed has loved you through the years. Give thanks to God for these graces.

December 18
Psalm 72:1,12-13,18-19
Matthew 1:18-24
(The angel and Joseph)

Joseph and Mary were betrothed when Mary became pregnant with Jesus. To Joseph, this indicated that Mary had been unfaithful, so he wanted to break off the relationship. This tradition and the story of the angelic appearance in today's reading give us a clue to the Messiah's identity: He is a child of the Holy Spirit.

- Look over the family tree you sketched yesterday and draw lines between yourself and those family members with whom you feel close. Write a comment about your relationship with each person next to your lines.

- Draw lines between yourself and those family members with whom you do not feel close. Write a comment about why you feel distant from each.

- Pray that the Messiah will come to your family this Christmas.

December 19
Psalm 71:3-6,16-17
Luke 1:5-25
(The origins of John the Baptist)

The story of Jesus is inseparable from that of John the Baptist. The two men were related through blood and through the Holy Spirit. The conception of John by the elderly Zechariah and Elizabeth brings to mind the conception and birth of Isaac and the nation of Israel by the aged Abraham and Sarah.

- Do you believe you are too old to change some of your ways?

- Spend some time with the words "In these days, the Lord is acting on my behalf." Let these words sink in. Try to believe them.

- How well are you handling Christmas preparations this year? Are you getting too caught up in the card-writing, gift-buying spirit?

December 20
Psalm 24:1-6
Luke 1:26-38
(The Annunciation)

Mary shall always occupy a unique place in salvation history. It was her acceptance of God's invitation that brought the Messiah into the world. She is a model for all who struggle to give birth to the Messiah in their own lives.

- How do you feel about Mary? What virtues does she model that appeal to you?

- Spend some time with the passage "Behold, I am the handmaid of the Lord. May it be done to me according to your word." Pray that this attitude will take deep root within you.

December 21
Psalm 33:2-3,11-12,20-21
Luke 1:39-45
(The Visitation)

It is always a sweet moment when we realize that other people understand our struggles and share our pain. Though years apart in age, Mary and Elizabeth share such a moment when Mary visits her wise cousin. Luke wrote about this joyful event for our edification.

- Think of a joyous statement to share with your family today. Resolve to share this joy.

- As Christmas approaches, charity in giving can fall prey to compulsion and last-minute sprees. How are you managing your shopping this year?

December 22
1 Samuel 2:1,4-8
Luke 1:46-56
(Mary's Magnificat)

The Magnificat is one of the most profound prayers in the Bible, summing up salvation history and important Old Testament revelations about God. Luke shows Mary uttering these words because she is the one upon whom God has bestowed the responsibility of bearing the Messiah.

• Spend a few moments with each passage, letting the words speak to you and your life situation. Stay with the passages that move you.

• Pray for the grace to praise God.

December 23
Psalm 25:4-5,8-10,14
Luke 1:57-66
(Zechariah names his son)

Jews believed that a person's name influenced the development of his or her character. They believed that to know a person's name was to have entry into that person's soul. The story of the naming of John the Baptist points out the influence of God in the life of this last Jewish prophet.

• How did you get your name? What qualities of character does your name suggest to you?

• Look in the mirror sometime today and tell yourself, "God doesn't make junk." Smile at yourself and pray for the grace to love yourself.

• Spend some time with the passage "The hand of the Lord was [is] with him [me]."

December 24
Psalm 89:2-5,27,29
Luke 1:67-79
(Zechariah's Canticle)

Just as he did in Mary's Magnificat, Luke writes of salvation history in Zechariah's Canticle. This prayer, used daily in the *Liturgy of the Hours*, is an inspiring statement about God's love for us, a prayer rich in meaning concerning both John the Baptist and us.

- Read through this passage slowly, spending time with the verses that move you. Write your impressions in your journal.

- Christmas Day is tomorrow. Will charity prevail? How will you celebrate the Incarnation?

The Season
of Christmas

Christ has come, and the world can never again be the same. During the days that follow, we will reflect upon several events that describe the meaning of the Incarnation. We will be invited to continue the journey we began in Advent, though now we walk with a new appreciation of the tremendous grace that has come to us in Jesus Christ.

December 26
Psalm 31:3-4,6-8,17,21
Matthew 10:17-22
(Stephen's martyrdom)

Recent studies have shown that the placement of this feast day in the Church's liturgical calendar has little to do with its proximity to Christmas. Yet Stephen's martyrdom reminds us that crucifixion is the price paid for incarnation. Today's gospel emphasizes this truth; it also promises glory for those who, like Stephen, are faithful to the end.

- In what ways do you die for Christ each day? How do these deaths to self allow the incarnation to happen in your life?

- Do you believe that you, at this point in your life, would be willing to die for your faith? Why? Why not?

- Pray for the grace to be willing to suffer for the sake of love.

December 27
Psalm 97:1-2,5-6,11-12
John 20:2-8
(John, apostle and evangelist)

In contrast to the martyrdom of the youthful Stephen, John the apostle is said to have lived to be a very old man. He alone of the apostles escaped violent martyrdom, showing the early Church it was possible to persevere in charity until a ripe old age—perhaps a more difficult challenge. His disciples left us a magnificent gospel, a tribute to his belief which is described in today's passage.

- In your imagination, journey with Peter and the beloved disciple to the tomb of Jesus. Note their shortness of breath as they arrive; feel their wonder as they venture inside, only to find the tomb vacated.

- Do you believe that Jesus Christ rose from the dead?

- Pray for the grace to be open to new life.

December 28
Psalm 124:2-5, 7-8
Matthew 2:13-18
(Holy Innocents, martyrs)

In today's reading we commemorate an event almost too horrible to believe. Tradition holds that Herod the Great, upon hearing of the birth of Jesus, the Messiah-king, was overcome with jealousy and ordered all infant boys in the Bethlehem area to be slain. This treachery is one of many examples of sin and wickedness which history records to help us recognize our need for salvation.

- How do you feel about the torturing of political prisoners and innocent victims in oppressive regimes? What is your response to this?

- Are you jealous of anyone or any group of people?

- Pray for the grace to be able to accept people just as they are.

December 29
Psalm 96:1-3, 5-6
Luke 2:22-35
(Jesus' consecration)

Always good Jews, Joseph and Mary are faithful in observing the Mosaic Law. Their consecration of

Jesus follows an ancient tradition. Simeon's words on this occasion describe some of the roles the Messiah is to play.

- What do you hope to accomplish and/or become before you die? What are you doing now to help realize this dream?

- What is it about your work that contributes to the building of God's kingdom on earth?

December 30
Psalm 96:7-10
Luke 2:36-40
(More prophecies about Jesus)

The religious heroes of all traditions usually come to us replete with mysterious origins and wonderful prophecies; stories about Jesus are no exception. It is said that Luke gathered much of the material for his infancy narratives from Mary, who had treasured the events of that time in her heart. Today's reading with Anna's prophecy may be one such event.

- How do you feel about the notion that Jesus grew in strength, grace, and wisdom?

- What are you doing to keep growing in your appreciation of the Church?

December 31
Psalm 96:1-2,11-13
John 1:1-18
(John's prologue)

Matthew and Luke provide genealogies which trace the human origins of Jesus back to David and Adam, respectively. John, however, proposes that the Word, who became flesh in Jesus, has existed with God from the beginning. This magnificent truth enables us to have a share of "love following upon love."

- Read slowly through this passage, spending time with the verses that move you. Write your reflections in your journal.

- Make a list of concrete, achievable resolutions for the new year by noting your responses to the question: "What would I like to see different in my life at this time next year?" For each response, write down a plan for achieving your objectives.

- Pray for openness to change during the coming year.

January 2
Psalm 98:1-4
John 1:19-28
(Jesus and John)

We now return to a familiar theme: John the Baptist is precursor to the Messiah. Like John, it is important that we, too, recognize our limitations.

- How does selfishness limit your experiences of creation, work, and relationships with other people?

- How do you usually respond to selfishness? Think about the next twenty-four hours and anticipate a time when selfishness will probably tempt you. Pray for the grace to respond in love.

January 3
Psalm 98:1-6
John 1:29-34
(The lamb of God)

Two important symbols describe the Messiah in today's reading. He is the Lamb of God whose sacrifice fulfills spiritually what the sacrificial lamb of Passover only anticipated. The dove is a symbol of the Holy Spirit, who rested upon the lamb, who animated Jesus.

- How do you feel about symbolic references to Jesus? Why do you think these symbols were important to John the Evangelist?

- In your imagination, picture yourself relaxing before a wellspring of flowing water. Pray that the Spirit may wash you clean of selfishness.

January 4
Psalm 98:1, 7-9
John 1:35-42
(John introduces Jesus)

John the Baptist perceives his role as pointing the way to Christ. Our life is to reflect this same virtue through our work, play, and relationships.

- Imagine you are a disciple of John, listening to him as he points out the Messiah. See Jesus walking along the Jordan River; notice him gazing at you with love. Follow him as he takes you to the place where he lives. See where he lives and be with him there.

- Pray for the grace to become more discerning of the many places where God lives.

January 5
Psalm 100:1-5
John 1:43-51
(Jesus, Philip, and Nathanael)

The calling of the apostles is one of the most revered of Christian traditions. Today's reading recalls the traditions surrounding the call of Philip and of Nathanael, probably identified in the other gospels as the apostle Bartholomew.

- How has God called you to be a follower of Jesus Christ? Who were his instruments? Recall the occasions that were turning points for you.

- How and why did you choose to become involved with the community of which you are now a member? Do you feel open to inviting others to join? Why? Why not?

January 6
Psalm 147:12-15,19-20
Mark 1:7-11
(Jesus is baptized by John)

Even though many people believed that John the Baptist was the Messiah, John certainly knew his place. The gospel traditions concerning the Baptist and Jesus preserve a healthy respect for the unique mission and charismatic ministry of John while pointing out that the ministry of Jesus in the Holy Spirit transcends that of John.

- Do you believe you have been baptized in the Holy Spirit? What does this term mean to you?

- Spend some time with the verse "You are my beloved [son/daughter]. With you I am well pleased." Pray for the grace to really feel God's favor.

January 7
Psalm 149:1-6,9
John 2:1-12
(The wedding at Cana)

Jewish weddings are joyous occasions, and Jesus seems to have enjoyed these festivities as much, or more, than anyone. The miracle of the transformed water symbolizes much more than his attempt to keep a party going, however; it points to the "new wine" which the Spirit produces in us and the wine poured out in the Eucharist, the gift of his flesh and blood.

- Is it hard for you to imagine Jesus having a good time? Is it hard for you to allow yourself to have fun?

- What does marriage mean to you? If you are married, let your spouse know today how important he or she is to you.

- Spend some time with the verse "Do whatever he tells you," Mary's stance toward Jesus. Invite God to speak to you in your thoughts.

Week After Epiphany

Monday (or January 7)
Psalm 2:7-8,10-11
Matthew 4:12-17,23-25
(Jesus heals)

Matthew's Gospel was addressed to a Jewish-Christian community, often quoting Old Testament prophets to show how Jesus fulfilled their predictions. In today's reading we learn that a world in darkness has been visited by a healing Messiah.

- Does the phrase "a land overshadowed by death" describe your perception of the world today? How does Christ's light help illuminate our world?

- Pray for the grace to be a source of healing to those around you today.

Tuesday (or January 8)
Psalm 72:1-4,7-8
Mark 6:34-44
(Jesus feeds thousands)

Jesus is no mere spiritual Messiah. His concern for our spiritual well-being is matched by his understanding of the importance of our bodily needs. He knows well that hungry people are not overly interested in theology, so he feeds them bread and fish.

- Spend some time with the passage "Give them some food yourselves." How do you feel about being a co-redeemer with Christ?

- What kind of responsibility do you feel toward the poor and hungry in your community?

Wednesday (or January 9)
Psalm 72:1-2,10,12-13
Mark 6:45-52
(Jesus on the water)

Because he wrote to Gentiles, Mark emphasized miraculous events surrounding the ministry of Jesus; his audience had little appreciation for Jewish prophecy and its fulfillment in Christ. In today's passage we read about one of the more unusual traditions preserved by the Church: Jesus' walk on the water. Rather than be overawed by the accomplishment of this feat, we should try to appreciate the symbolic meanings conveyed by Mark.

- Why did Jesus spend time alone in prayer? Do you believe he had human needs just as we do?

- Spend some time with the verse "Take courage, it is I, do not be afraid!" Let these words bring peace to your soul. Call them to mind through the day.

Thursday (or January 10)
Psalm 72:1-2,14-15,17
Luke 4:14-22
(Jesus at Nazareth)

The Jewish synagogue was the place where people from the local community gathered to worship. As part of the service, people from the congregation were invited to read Scripture passages. Frequently the president of the synagogue invited distinguished guests to comment on the passages. It was often from that forum that Jesus addressed the Jews.

- Although Jesus obviously disagreed with the manner in which many aspects of Judaism were taught, he still went to the synagogue to worship with the people. What does this say to you about community and worship?

- Spend some time with the verse "The Spirit of the Lord is upon me, / because he has anointed me." Pray for the grace to believe these words.

Friday (or January 11)
Psalm 147:12-15,19-20
Luke 5:12-16
(Jesus cures a leper)

Today medical treatment effectively controls leprosy, but during the time of Christ and until recently, the disease affected many. Because some forms are contagious, people who had leprosy were cast out of the community and were required to cry "Unclean!" when anyone approached. In isolation with other lepers, they were left to rot away. Only against this background can we appreciate the significance of Jesus' contact with lepers.

- How do you feel about your contact with lower classes of society? Do you avoid such contacts?
- How is lack of discipline causing you to rot away spiritually? Ask Jesus to cure you.

Saturday (or January 12)
Psalm 149:1-6,9
John 3:22-30
(John points to Jesus)

On this last day of the Advent-Christmas-Epiphany season, we again listen to the words of John the Baptist. "He must increase, I must decrease," John says, reflecting an attitude we should all take if the light of the Messiah is to become incarnate in our lives and transform this world.

- "The glory of God is humanity fully alive," Irenaeus wrote. Do you believe that this is an important statement about Incarnation? Are you a fully alive person?

- Resolve to pay more attention to the vibrant people you meet today. Ask what the secret is to their vitality.

Ordinary Time
After Christmas

We now begin the longest season of the liturgical year: Ordinary Time. Depending upon the date of Easter, five to seven weeks of this season precede Lent. During this time we will move more or less systematically through the Gospels of Mark, Matthew, and Luke, respectively, focusing our attention on the "ordinary" ministry of Jesus between his baptism and crucifixion.

First Week
in Ordinary Time

Monday
Psalm 97:1-2,6-7,9
Mark 1:14-20
(Jesus begins his ministry)

Mark's account of Jesus' early proclamation gives us a preview of all that is to follow. Jesus sees himself and his ministry as essential for the coming of God's reign. He invites us to reform our lives if we, too, are to be citizens of this kingdom.

- What is so good about the Good News? How is it different from other news?

- What kind of man must Jesus have been to attract four fishermen away from their tasks? Picture the call of these apostles in your imagination. Hear Jesus calling you, too, to follow him.

Tuesday
Psalm 8:2,5-9
Mark 1:21-28
(An exorcism)

The people of Jesus' time believed that myriad evil spirits ruled the earth. Some of these spirits, they believed, were angels who had fallen from grace, while others were evil people who had died. Jesus' healings were thus understood in terms of displacing an evil spirit with the Holy Spirit.

- What kind of evil spirit keeps you from loving yourself as God loves you? What changes in yourself and/or the circumstances in which you live would make it easier for you to love yourself? Make a plan to begin working toward these changes.

- Spend some time with the verse "What have you to do with [me], Jesus of Nazareth?" Listen to your thoughts as Jesus responds.

Wednesday
Psalm 105:1-4,6-9
Mark 1:29-3
(A full day of ministering)

The healing of Simon Peter's mother-in-law shows us that Jesus did not heal only to impress the masses. He extends his healing touch because people need healing. He travels the countryside to touch many.

- Jesus' day was a mixture of solitude and action. Do you believe there is a good balance between these disciplines in your own life? How can you better balance them?

- Pray for the grace to be more willing to share yourself with others.

Thursday
Psalm 95:6-11
Mark 1:40-45
(Jesus cures a leper)

The gospels do not include a single instance when Jesus refuses to heal someone who requests wholeness. The prayer of the leper in today's reading should be a model for all of us because the leper makes his request in great humility and leaves the matter in Jesus' hands.

- Do you believe that God answers your prayers? What kinds of prayers do you find answered most often?

- What are some reasons why you are usually afraid to reach out to others? Pray for the grace to overcome these resistances.

Friday
Psalm 78:3-4,6-8
Mark 2:1-12
(Jesus can forgive sins)

The Scriptures teach us that sin is a power which keeps us from growing and which breaks up relationships. In today's reading Jesus shows us that he can heal us from physical and spiritual paralysis.

- Some theologians have stated that we sin most often not by doing malicious and destructive things but by settling for less than the best in ourselves. Think about this.

- What is paralyzing your love for family members? Pray for the grace to overcome any obstacles.

Saturday
Psalm 19:8-10,15
Mark 2:13-17
(An early confrontation)

People loved Jesus and large crowds followed him. He was successful in attracting a group as diverse as fishermen, tax collectors, prostitutes, and even a member of the Sanhedrin. This success provoked jealousy among Jewish authorities and led many of them to self-righteous judgments.

- Do you feel a need for God in your life? Why? Why not? What do you need God to do for you?
- What are the fruits of self-righteousness? Do any of these appear in your life?

Second Week in Ordinary Time

Monday
Psalm 110:1-4
Mark 2:18-22
(On new wine and new cloth)

Jealousy prompts the Pharisees and the disciples of John to try to find fault with Jesus' spirituality. Rather than return the criticism, as he could have done, Jesus invites them to be open to a new way of doing God's will.

- Gibran said that Jesus stood before the world as the first man stood on the first day. Are you open to seeing the world in its daily newness?

- Resolve to stop many times today to appreciate creation and the people around you. Give thanks to God for these gifts. Begin now.

Tuesday
Psalm 111:1-2,4-5,9-10
Mark 2:23-28
(Jesus, Lord of the Sabbath)

In Deuteronomy 23:26, it is stated that Jews may pluck "some of the ears with your hand, but do not put a sickle to your neighbor's grain." This prevented the poor and starving from going hungry, but it was never to be done on the Sabbath. Jesus shows us that human needs are more important than a rigid interpretation of the law.

- Do you go to church out of a sense of obligation? Evaluate your motives.

- How is Jesus the lord of your Sunday experience?

Wednesday
Psalm 110:1-4
Mark 3:1-6
(A healing and a confrontation)

Today's reading describes a significant turning point in the ministry of Jesus. Jewish law forbade medical ministry on the Sabbath except in critical life-saving situations. The man with the paralyzed hand is not in critical condition, but Jesus heals him anyway. Because of this act of love, he earns the contempt of the legalistic Pharisees.

- Picture this confrontation in your imagination. Note the anger and indignation on Jesus' face as he addresses the authorities; see them responding to him from the heights of self-righteousness; experience the thrill of the moment when Jesus overrides the Sabbath restrictions by saying, "Stretch out your hand." Note the gratitude on the man's face as his hand is healed.

- Are you self-assured yet humble in your efforts to love others?

Thursday
Psalm 40:7-10,17
Mark 3:7-12
(Jesus and the crowds)

Again and again Mark writes of the crowds who followed Jesus for healing, teaching, and out of curiosity. Withdrawing from areas where conflict with the authorities might bring a premature end to his ministry, Jesus takes to the countryside, pursued by the crowds. He ministers on, undaunted.

- An ancient story tells of Satan instructing evil spirits in the art of damning souls. The most successful temptation was not to deny God's existence, or even the devil's existence, but "There's plenty of time." Why is this attitude so damning? Would you search for Jesus out in the "countryside"?

- Spend some time with the words of the psalmist: "Be still and confess that I am God!" (Psalm 46:11).

Friday
Psalm 85:10-14
Mark 3:13-19
(Jesus chooses the Twelve)

Gospel parallels between Jesus and Moses are surely not coincidental. Moses went up on the mountain and brought back God's laws to the twelve tribes of Israel. Jesus goes to the mountaintop and returns with twelve men empowered to extend his healing love to a broken world.

- William Barclay noted that the apostles had no special gifts of intelligence or literacy, but they all loved Jesus and were willing to stand up for his cause. Are these qualities true of you?

- What kind of power does Jesus enable you to realize and extend?

- Thank God for the grace of being a disciple of Jesus Christ.

Saturday
Psalm 47:2-3,6-9
Mark 3:20-21
(Jesus and his family)

The family of Jesus undoubtedly had heard time and again of his extraordinary lifestyle, and they were undoubtedly concerned about his sanity. How painful for him and for them is their attempt to take charge of him. God's call sometimes takes us to lonely places!

- Are you waiting for someone's approval before you get on with your life?

- Thoreau wrote that most people "live lives of quiet desperation." Do you believe this is true?

- Pray for the grace to be willing to break out of the confines of oppressive conventionalities.

Third Week
in Ordinary Time

Monday
Psalm 98:1-6
Mark 3:22-30
(Sin against the Spirit)

Today's gospel shows Jesus confronting the scribes and their criticism of his exorcisms. Never one to back down from an opportunity to clarify God's truth, Jesus exposes the illogic of their arguments and issues that terrible warning about sinning against the Spirit, about refusing to let the Spirit work in us.

- What would you like the Holy Spirit to help you to do and be? Ask God to help you to claim this grace.

- Jesus never backed away from a chance to teach. Are there times in your life when you could speak out more boldly for the sake of the kingdom?

Tuesday
Psalm 40:2,4,7-8,10-11
Mark 3:31-35
(The true relatives of Jesus)

Unlike the other evangelists, Mark does not apologize for Jesus' family and their misunderstanding of his mission. They have come to take him home, presumably to try to talk some sense into him. Jesus responds by claiming that he owes more allegiance to the family of God.

- How involved in family matters are you? Does your family identity complement or detract from your identity as a child of God?

- If you could change anything in your family, what would it be? For what are you most thankful?

Wednesday
Psalm 110:1-4
Mark 4:1-20
(Parable of the Sower)

Jesus tries to teach about spiritual matters by using analogies to human experiences. His parables are attempts to tease the mind into understanding his message.

- Apply this parable to your present situation, letting the seed be the Word of God and the field be your own heart rather than society.

- What are examples of footpaths, rocky ground, thorns, and fertile ground in your life? How can you better cultivate your field to give the Word fertile ground?

Thursday
Psalm 24:1-6
Mark 4:21-25
(Nothing is hidden from God)

Truth and love cannot be forever suppressed, Jesus tells us. Like light shining in darkness, the works of a disciple of Jesus will not remain hidden. It is precisely these works which will prevent the darkness of sin from completely overtaking the world.

- Emerson wrote, "Be careful of what you want, for you will get it." What are you really seeking in your everyday involvements? Why?
- Pray for the grace of purity of intention.

Friday
Psalm 37:3-6,23-24,39-40
Mark 4:26-34
(The mustard seed)

The kingdom of God will conquer, Jesus assures us, for God's will is sovereign. Grace reaches deeper than sin; evil will be uprooted.

- Do you believe you have made progress in your life in growing closer to Christ during the past few months? Years? How has grace transformed you?
- Do you feel hopeful about God's kingdom conquering evil? Why? Why not? How does this affect your everyday attitude?

Saturday
Luke 1:69-75
Mark 4:35-41
(Calming a storm)

This is a very human scene: Jesus sleeping, the disciples afraid of a storm at sea. Mark tells us that peace comes to the disciples when they realize that Jesus is with them.

- Over what storms in your life would you like the peace of God to reign?
- Spend some time to allow the admonition "Quiet! Be Still!" deepen your peace.

Fourth Week in Ordinary Time

Monday
Psalm 31:20-24
Mark 5:1-20
(Exorcising a hopeless case)

Jesus has ventured into an area inhabited by non-Jews. This story of the demoniac and the swineherd reminds us that Jesus has come to save all people, even the lowest of classes and the most hopeless of cases. The price of a human soul is worth more to God than anything else in the world.

- Let your imagination re-create this scene for you. How did Jesus look at the demoniac? Hear him saying to you, "Unclean spirits, be gone!"

- What kind of involvement do you have with the poor, the underprivileged, and the outcasts of society?

Tuesday
Psalm 22:26-32
Mark 5:21-43
(More healings and resuscitations)

Jesus never refuses anyone's request for healing. His miraculous deeds demonstrate the presence of the kingdom of God in the midst of humanity. Today's reading reveals God's desire to make people whole.

- The woman touched Jesus in such a manner that she drew power from him. Why did Jesus want to know who touched him?

- Has anyone ever touched you or someone you know with expectant faith? How did each of you respond?

Wednesday
Psalm 103:1-2,13-14,17-18
Mark 6:1-6
(Jesus rejected by his own)

The response of the people of Nazareth to Jesus teaches us an important lesson. They think they know him and they try to make him conform to their own ideas. Consequently, they fail to recognize him for who he is, and he is unable to touch them. We, too, need to be cautious about thinking we know and understand Jesus completely.

- Louis Evely once wrote, "As soon as we think we know someone, we have ceased to love them." How does this relate to the people of Nazareth? How does it relate to your relationship with Jesus? With your family and friends?
- Pray for the grace to discover newness in God, in yourself, and in others.

Thursday
Psalm 48:2-4,9-11
Mark 6:7-13
(The Twelve sent out)

It is important to note that Jesus sends the apostles out in pairs. From the beginning, the importance of support in ministry has been emphasized, as well as traveling light, free from unnecessary burdens. Simplicity of lifestyle and fellowship in community remain important values for Christians.

- Do you have a simple lifestyle? What adjustments do you feel are necessary so that you might experience the freedom that the simple life offers?

- Do you have the support you need to minister in your daily life? Pray for the grace to experience support from friends.

Friday
Psalm 27:1,3,5,8-9
Mark 6:14-29
(Herod and John)

Herod had tried to silence the voice of his own conscience by imprisoning and killing John the Baptist. This passage points out the utter superficiality of Herod's life and issues a subtle warning about the impossibility of suppressing God's intentions.

- Herod was trapped in a role, unable to find holiness because of his life situation. How are you like him? How are you different?

- Pray for the grace to break out of roles that confine you.

Saturday
Psalm 23:1-6
Mark 6:30-34
(The people ruin a retreat)

Jesus sees that his tired band of disciples need to get away to be with him. He tries to take them on a private "retreat" but finds his plans frustrated. Note the manner in which he readjusts his concern.

- How do you usually respond to interruptions and frustrated plans? Do you see them as occasions to minister?

- Review your plans for today and anticipate times when they might go awry. How will you respond?
- Pray for the grace to recognize opportunities to love and grow.

Fifth Week
in Ordinary Time

Monday
Psalm 104:1-2,5-6,10,12,24,35
Mark 6:53-56
(The people seek Jesus out)

Without the aid of television, radio, or newspaper advertisements, Jesus' reputation has spread. People have found in him one who can meet their needs, so they search for him.

- How convinced are you of your need of God? What do you need most from God?

- Spend time thanking God for graces you usually take for granted.

Tuesday
Psalm 8:4-9
Mark 7:1-13
(The injustice of certain traditions)

Although the Pharisees are constantly criticized in the gospels, they were popular religious leaders, similar in stature among their communities to today's parish priests. Their major fault lay in their legalistic observance of the Law, even to the point of hurting people or ignoring human needs in the process. Jesus points out a few examples of this in today's reading.

- Can you think of an example of legalism in your own experience in the Church? How does this affect your involvement in the Church now?

- What criteria did Jesus employ for evaluating the justice of a law?

Wednesday
Psalm 104:1-2,27-30
Mark 7:14-23
(On what makes for uncleanness)

Jewish dietary laws were initially established for a variety of reasons, many related more to health than to piety. It is because many Jews believed that holiness depended upon observing such rules and regulations, rather than being pure of heart, that Jesus criticizes the dietary law observances.

- Let your imagination take you to the recesses of your heart. What do you see there?

- Pray for the grace to recognize your mixed motives.

Thursday
Psalm 128:1-5
Mark 7:24-30
(Daughter of a Gentile woman healed)

Jesus' seemingly harsh rebuke to the woman is softened somewhat when we realize that the word he used for *dog* actually means "house pet." His confrontation with the woman draws a faith response from her while teaching his disciples that God's grace is for all people, not just Jews.

- What kind of demon is straining relationships in your family? What does love require to exorcise this demon?

- Pray for the grace to be more loving to family members.

Friday
Psalm 32:1-2,5-7
Mark 7:31-37
(Healing a deaf man)

Again we see Jesus encouraging people to be silent regarding a miracle. To Jesus, miracles are signs of the presence of God in our midst, and he does not want this to be misinterpreted on account of sensationalism.

- Is there anyone you know who needs to hear words of love from you but has not because of your hesitation to reach out?

- Hear Jesus saying, "Ephphatha! Be opened!" To what do you need to be more open?

Saturday
Psalm 90:2-6,12-13
Mark 8:1-10
(Second miracle of the loaves)

The multiplication of the loaves and fish is often considered a foreshadowing of the eucharistic Bread of Life. Just as Jesus gave sustenance to people through his teachings, healings, and miraculous feedings, so now does he continue to nourish us in a special way through his presence in the Eucharist.

- Make a list of the excuses you usually make to distance yourself from responding to the needs of the poor and hungry.

- Thank God for the grace of a substantial diet.

Sixth Week
in Ordinary Time

Monday
Psalm 50:1,8,16-17,20-21
Mark 8:11-13
(Pharisees seek a sign)

The Pharisees expected the Messiah to manifest certain glorious signs, and their request for such a sign from Jesus is an attempt to test him. Jesus rejects their request, hurt at their distrust and disturbed that their faith is so shallow.

- If you were to ask God to manifest some sign to deepen your faith, for what would you ask? How would this help you? What would it say about God?

- Pray for faith in God.

Tuesday
Psalm 29:1-4,9-10
Mark 8:14-21
(Jesus warns his disciples to be on guard)

Although Jesus' disciples loved him dearly, there were times when they found it hard to comprehend the symbolic language of their master. When Jesus tries to warn them about the influence of the Pharisees and Herod, they misinterpret his words. They really do not understand him.

- List a few destructive "yeasts" in our society that erode faith. With which of these do you struggle most intensely?

- Thank God for things which you have taken for granted recently.

Wednesday
Psalm 116:12-15,18-19
Mark 8:22-26
(Jesus heals a blind man)

In this passage we see Jesus giving individual attention to a man brought to him by the crowd. Similarly, we must remember that our God, who is present to all of creation, nevertheless gives each one of us his fullest attention.

- Leo Buscaglia said, "If you don't touch, you're out of touch." How do you feel about touching those you love? How do you feel about being touched?

- Re-create this gospel scene in your imagination. Hear Jesus saying, "Can you see anything?" Ask him to heal your blindnesses.

Thursday
Psalm 102:16-23,29
Mark 8:27-33
(Who do you say he is?)

This passage marks a turning point in Mark's Gospel. The community, through Peter, asserts its faith in Jesus as the Messiah and, in turn, challenges all people to answer this most important of all questions for themselves.

- Who do you say Jesus was/is? Why do you believe this?

- You may find it helpful to write a short letter to Jesus. Thank him for being who he is for you.

Friday
Psalm 33:10-15
Mark 8:34–9:1
(The way of the cross)

Following the way of loving service will not always be easy, Jesus promises. But those who persevere in love, even through times of suffering, will become a new creation.

- What does the cross mean to you? How do you experience it in your life?

- What does it mean to "lose your life" for the sake of the gospel?

Saturday
Psalm 145:2-5,10-11
Mark 9:2-13
(Christ's glory revealed)

In a moment of profound intimacy, the core leadership of the apostles—Peter, James, and John—glimpses the depths of Jesus' heart. They recognize in him the fulfillment of the Law and the prophets and hear the call to obey him as their lord. Jesus, who had recently promised them the cross, now gives them a promise of the glory to come.

- Have you ever felt as Peter, James, and John must have felt on the mountain of transfiguration? Try to recall the circumstances and invite those feelings to renew you.

- Spend time with the passage "This is my beloved Son. Listen to him." After a few moments, write down what you think Jesus is telling you.

Seventh Week
in Ordinary Time

Monday
Psalm 93:1-2,5
Mark 9:14-29
(Jesus cures an epileptic)

The pathology of epilepsy is no longer explained as demonic possession as it was during Jesus' time. His healing of the epileptic boy was considered an exorcism since medical science did not yet understand this illness. This healing is yet another example of Jesus' desire to make people whole.

- Re-create in your imagination the scene between the father and Jesus. Hear Jesus saying, "Everything is possible for anyone who has faith."

- Make a commitment to a day of prayer and fasting for one day this week to deepen your relationship with God and others.

Tuesday
Psalm 37: 3-4,18-19,27-28,39-40
Mark 9:30-37
(On true greatness)

Jesus continually tried to tell his disciples that their understanding of the Messiah must include suffering and service. In today's reading he counters their notions of esteem by lauding the simplicity of a child.

- What does greatness mean to you? What would you have to accomplish to consider yourself great?

- What do the words and gestures of Jesus with the child tell us about God's standards of greatness?
- Pray for the grace of humility.

Wednesday
Psalm 119:165,168,171-172,174-175
Mark 9:38-40
(The name of Jesus)

In biblical times names were considered important because they gave identity and a claim upon a person. Using the name of Jesus to exorcise a demon meant calling on the Power whom Jesus invoked in healing.

- How do you feel when other people speak about their relationship with God in a way that seems strange to you? Are you tolerant of them?
- What does it mean to be against Jesus? What are some manifestations of this?

Thursday
Psalm 1:1-4,6
Mark 9:41-50
(Commitment and responsibility)

The gospels show Jesus becoming most infuriated at those in leadership positions—parents, teachers, and ministers—who lead the naive and ignorant astray for self-serving reasons. Today's reading expresses the seriousness of Christian responsibility.

- Were you ever scandalized by an adult's behavior when you were younger? How did you handle it then? How has this affected you?
- Pray for the grace to have "salt in yourself," to know that you are loved by God.

Friday
Psalm 119:12,16,18,27,34-35
Mark 10:1-12
(On marriage and divorce)

In a culture that permitted a man to leave his wife for the slightest excuse (though not vice versa), Jesus' words on the seriousness of the marriage commitment are ill-received. He believes, however, that love relationships cannot grow without commitment. These words shall forever be challenging.

- What is the value of commitment in a love relationship? Do you believe that God is committed to you?

- Spend time thanking God for those people in your life who are committed to loving you.

Saturday
Psalm 103:13-18
Mark 10:13-16
(Jesus and the children)

In the non-Jewish communities to whom Mark wrote, children were not recognized as persons with rights. They were often beaten and neglected; infanticide was not uncommon; abortion was accepted. Jesus' love of children challenges these attitudes and reveals something very special about God.

- What does it mean to you to accept God's kingdom as a little child? Does this describe your attitude?

- What are you doing to help alleviate the suffering of children in poor and oppressed countries?

Eighth Week
in Ordinary Time

Monday
Psalm 32:1-2,5-7
Mark 10:17-27
(The danger of riches)

It is noteworthy that Jesus never condemned material goods—not even money and alcohol. His confrontation with the rich young man warns us, however, that the love of material goods can keep us from growing spiritually.

- Let your imagination re-create this encounter between Jesus and the rich young man. See Jesus looking at him with love; hear him challenge the young man to live a life of poverty and freedom; observe how the young man's face grows sad.

- Why did Jesus challenge the rich young man to give away his goods? Do you believe everyone is called to do this? Are you?

- Pray for the grace to be less attached to material goods.

Tuesday
Psalm 50:5-8,14,23
Mark 10:28-31
(The last shall be first)

Many people today believe that the rewards for a follower of Jesus are reserved for the next life. But Jesus promises that following him will also bring blessings in this life, though not without suffering.

- Do you believe that following Jesus is the best way to live your life? Why? Why not?
- What are some rewards you experience from following Jesus? What are some of the sufferings?
- Thank God for the gift of life.

Wednesday
Psalm 79:8-9,11,13
Mark 10:32-45
(On servant leadership)

Mark again contrasts Jesus' notion of the messiah as a suffering servant with the apostles' ambitions and vanities. Jesus explains that a commitment to service is the only way to guarantee that leadership does not go to one's head.

- Many have written that the proper attitude for a Christian is expressed thus: "What can I do to help?" Do you agree? Does this saying summarize your attitude toward people and circumstances?
- Review your day to come and anticipate times when you will need grace to be more loving. Ask for this grace.

Thursday
Psalm 33:2-9
Mark 10:46-52
(Bold faith and prayer)

Time and again Jesus changed his plans so he could help someone in need. In today's reading he restores sight to a blind man—one who lived by begging. Bartimaeus, the blind man, shows us the value of boldly asking for grace.

- Spend some time with the verse "What do you want me to do for you?" What is your reply?
- Pray for a deepening faith.

Friday
Psalm 149:1-6,9
Mark 11:11-26
(The withered fig tree)

Old Testament prophets sometimes compared the people of Israel to trees, branches, and vines. Today's stories of the withered fig tree and the cleansing of the Temple show Jesus confronting the barrenness of the Jews of his day, a barrenness stemming from their failure to receive his teaching and their failure to understand the meaning of true worship.

- How do you feel about Jesus' actions in this passage? Is it possible for anger to serve love?
- What occurred in the temple of your soul during the past day?

Saturday
Psalm 19:8-11
Mark 11:27-33
(The authority of Jesus)

Jesus' cleansing of the Temple was daring and provocative. When a deputation comes to trap him by asking for his credentials for doing this, Jesus sees through their trap. He sidesteps their charges of blasphemy and arrogance by exposing their complicities concerning John the Baptist.

- Have you ever compromised your perception of truth because you were fearful of others' opinions? Have you done so recently?

- Preview your day and anticipate a time when you will have an opportunity to say or do something to further Christian truth. Resolve to do something when that time comes.
- Pray for the grace to speak the truth lovingly.

The Season
of Lent

During Lent we continue to reflect upon the mysteries celebrated during Advent and Christmas. The Incarnation of God in the person of Jesus Christ is made fully manifest through Jesus' suffering, death, and resurrection. To help us prepare properly to reverence Jesus as lord and savior, the Church encourages prayer, fasting, and mortification of self-indulgent passions. In recent years the importance of acts of love and mercy has also been emphasized.

Ash Wednesday
Psalm 51:3-6,12-14,17
Mark 6:1-6,16-18
(Be sincere)

Gaining the esteem of others is something we all desire. But Jesus makes it clear that our religious acts should be done to bring us closer to God, not to impress people. Some of the examples of hypocrisy he gives refer to practices of the Pharisees.

- How important is it to you that others know you are committed to following Jesus Christ? What are your motives for letting others know that you are a Christian?

- In what ways does your heavenly Father repay you for your prayer in private? Spend some time thanking God for these graces.

Thursday After Ash Wednesday
Psalm 1:1-4,6
Luke 9:22-25
(Take up your cross)

Jesus tries to help his disciples realize that his commitment to love will lead him into a fatal conflict with the authorities of his day. Dying to ourselves for the sake of love will lead us, with Jesus, to new life.

- Make a list of some of the attributes of the old self which you need to change for the sake of love. Which of these attributes most frustrates your efforts at loving?

- Pray for the grace to change destructive behaviors.

Friday After Ash Wednesday
Psalm 51:3-6,18-19
Matthew 9:14-15
(Jesus the bridegroom)

Often Jesus likens God's kingdom to a wedding feast where people rejoice and have fun. The day will come, however, when fasting is appropriate. That time is now.

- Read Isaiah 58:1-9, today's first reading, to better understand the kind of fast God desires. How can you practice this spirit of fasting?

- Pray to hunger for the things of God.

Saturday After Ash Wednesday
Psalm 86:1-6
Luke 5:27-32
(The call of Levi)

Tax collectors were men commissioned by the Romans to exact from the peoples they governed monies and property owed Rome. Then, as now, tax collectors were despised by the people. Levi, a Jew, was considered a traitor by other Jews. Nevertheless, Jesus chooses him to be a disciple, a member of his inner circle. Jesus' call elicits gratitude from Levi and scandalizes the Pharisees and scribes.

- What does Jesus mean when he talks of healthy and sick people? In what group do you consider yourself? How are you sick? How are you healthy?

- Spend some time re-creating this scene in your imagination. Sense the rejection Levi feels from his fellow Jews; note a change when he sees Jesus paying attention to him; hear Jesus saying to him, and to you, "Follow me."

First Week
in Lent

Monday
Psalm 19:8-10,15
Matthew 25:31-46
(Who are the saved?)

It is often said that the clearest indication of our relationship with God can be determined by our relationships with human beings. In today's reading Jesus makes it clear that we will be judged on the basis of how we have treated others—even the outcasts of society.

- If you were to die today, do you think you would be included in the company of the sheep or of the goats?

- Is there any person or any racial or religious group against whom you harbor resentments and harsh judgments?

- Pray for the grace to see all people as children of God.

Tuesday
Psalm 34:4-7,16-19
Matthew 6:7-15
(The Lord's Prayer)

This most famous of all prayers is a formula for prayer, including movements of acknowledgment of God as creator, praise, hope for the kingdom, affirmation of the importance of life on earth, petition for our needs, requests for forgiveness, and protection from evil. This passage concludes with a sobering reminder that our experience of God's forgiveness is contingent upon our own willingness to forgive.

- Spend a few moments with each line of the Lord's Prayer, adding your own prayers to each verse. When you ask for your daily bread and for forgiveness, be specific in your requests.

Wednesday
Psalm 51:3-4,12-13,18-19
Luke 11:29-32
(The sign of Jonah)

Jesus' condemnation of the attitude of the crowds is intended to move them to faith. He sees that they do not really hunger for the things of God but want demonstrations of supernatural power instead. The Queen of Sheba and the Ninevites were pagans who recognized the workings of God in holy Jews and reformed their lives accordingly. Jesus holds them out as models to us.

- What are some signs of God's presence that are most meaningful to you? What are signs you need to try harder to recognize?

- Pray for the grace to recognize God's workings in yourself and others.

Thursday
Psalm 138:1-3, 7-8
Matthew 7:7-12
(Ask, seek, knock)

Jesus reveals a God who is generous and responsive. This does not exempt us from searching for ways to grow closer to him. It is in searching and asking that we discover ourselves and God's goodness.

- What are you seeking from God? From your family members?

- How would you like others to treat you? Make a list, then commit yourself to treating others likewise.

Friday
Psalm 130:1-8
Matthew 5:20-26
(On forgiveness and reconciliation)

Today's reading introduces an important lesson. We learn that anger can separate us from others and thus we ought to control it by striving to be reconciled with those who are the objects of our anger.

- What (or who) most often causes your anger? How do you usually handle your anger? Are your expectations about others always reasonable? How can you change them?

- Make a commitment to reconcile with someone with whom you're angry (or who is angry with you).

Saturday
Psalm 119:1-2, 4-5, 7-8
Matthew 5:43-48
(Love your enemies)

Jesus teaches that the only way to break the seemingly never-ending cycle of hatred and revenge is to begin to treat enemies as fellow children of God. The commandment to love our enemies is one of the most unique of all Jesus' teachings and, unfortunately, the most neglected.

- Voltaire wrote that patriotism really means hating every other country but your own. Do you sense this kind of spirit in the world around you? How does it affect you?

- Spend some time praying for people with whom you do not get along particularly well. Ask for the grace to begin to love them.

Second Week in Lent

Monday
Psalm 79:8-9,11,13
Luke 6:36-38
(Do not judge)

Today's reading is one of the most sobering in Scripture. Jesus proposes that we evaluate our lives using the same criteria we use to evaluate others. How do we fare?

- Old sayings proclaim "What goes around comes around" and "You will get out of life no more nor less than you put into it." Are these true in your experience?

- Why are Christians called to be compassionate?

- Pray for the grace to see others as God sees them.

Tuesday
Psalm 50:8-9,16-17,21,23
Matthew 23:1-12
(On servant leadership)

The principle of servant leadership holds that one's ability to use authority responsibly is directly related to one's service to others. Authority assumed for reasons other than service will result in many kinds of abuse and superficialities.

- Which title best fits Jesus: king, ruler, servant, master, prophet, teacher, philosopher, rabbi? Why did you choose the answer you did?

- Do you think of yourself as a servant? Whom do you serve?

Wednesday
Psalm 31:5-6,14-16
Matthew 20:17-28
(A mother's request)

It is obvious to us today that the mother of Zebedee's sons does not understand what Jesus' kingdom is about. Her request is made in good faith—not an unusual one from a Jewish mother trying to insure that her sons get the best treatment possible. The indignation which follows is turned into a teachable moment by Jesus.

- What are some of your professional ambitions? How important is it to you that you realize them? Why?

- Pray for the grace to accept failures as gracefully as successes.

Thursday
Psalm 1:1-4,6
Luke 16:19-31
(The rich man and Lazarus)

The parable of the rich man and Lazarus teaches us that the real value of our lives must be seen against a backdrop of the inevitability of death and the prospect of judgment by God. The surest way to guarantee repose in the "bosom of Abraham" is to love God and neighbor.

- What situations make you feel insecure? When do you feel most secure? What is your primary source of security?

- How do you feel about the prospect of evaluating your life before God after your death?

Friday
Psalm 105:16-21
Matthew 21:33-43,45-46
(Parable of the wicked tenants)

Jesus did not hide behind polite facades when love required that truth be spoken. In today's parable he reveals his knowledge of the intentions of Jewish authorities to dispose of him, yet he continues to invite them to recognize God working through him.

- God has entrusted us with the cultivation of a vineyard, his kingdom. Who are the faithful tenants today? Who are the unfaithful ones? How can you tell one from the other?

- If the Master of the vineyard were to come today, what do you think he would say to you? Spend some time listening.

Saturday
Psalm 103:1-4,9-12
Luke 15:1-3,11-32
(The Prodigal Son)

Today's parable is extremely rich in meaning. The marked contrasts between the attitudes of the father, the faithful son, and the prodigal son tell us much about God and ourselves.

- List some of the areas in your life where you are faithful to God. Also give a few of the reasons *why* you are faithful in each of those areas.

- Write a short characterization of the father in the parable.
- Pray for the grace to know that you are a forgiven sinner.

Third Week in Lent

Monday
Psalm 42:2-3;43:3-4
Luke 4:24-30
(A confrontation in Nazareth)

Since Jesus grew up in Nazareth, it is understandable that the people of this town think they know him better than most. They can not accept his special ministry, however, so Jesus confronts them for their lack of faith.

- Have you ever felt boxed-in or limited by close friends and family members who are interested only in that part of you with which they are comfortable? What is your response to this?

- Is there some friend or family member whom you need to get to know better? Make a commitment to communicate with that person about something new this week.

Tuesday
Psalm 25:4-9
Matthew 18:21-35
(The depths of forgiveness)

Today's reading continues to develop a theme that runs through the entire Lenten season: forgiveness and reconciliation. Jesus' admonition to forgive seventy-seven or seventy times seven times is not to be taken literally, of course; Jesus is simply using exaggeration to make an important point.

- Is there someone whom you need to forgive? Ask for guidance to think of a creative way to let that person know that you forgive him or her.

- Is there someone in your life whom you feel owes you forgiveness? Is reconciliation with this person possible?

Wednesday
Psalm 147:12-16,19-20
Matthew 5:17-19
(God's commandments are eternal)

Jesus teaches that God's commandments are not given to us to analyze or to evaluate their worth in terms of our own desires. Rather, God's commandments are given to help form our desires; these laws are to be obeyed.

- With which of God's commandments do you struggle most often? How will this struggle probably take place today?

- Pray for the grace to become more obedient to God's commandments.

Thursday
Psalm 95:1-2,6-9
Luke 11:14-23
(The reign of God is upon you)

The gospels reveal that it is impossible for people to encounter Jesus and remain indifferent toward him. This passage shows that some people interpret his influence and power as arising from demonic sources. Jesus exposes the irrationality of their accusation and invites them to join him in gathering the kingdom harvest.

- What do you believe it means to be "with" Jesus? Whom do you believe is with him?

- What kind of conscience guards the door of your soul? List some of the values that are most important to you.

Friday
Psalm 81:6-11,14,17
Mark 12:28-34
(The greatest commandment)

True religion is much simpler than we usually make it. In this passage Jesus teaches us that God is not a philosophical proposition to be figured out but rather a being to be loved. Likewise, other human beings are to be loved even as we love ourselves.

- Make a list of the people and things you love most in this world, ranking them according to their importance to you. Where does God come in? How can you draw closer to God?

- Do you love yourself? How does your self-love affect your relationships?

Saturday
Psalm 51:3-4,18-21
Luke 18:9-14
(The Pharisee and the Publican)

In this parable of contrasts, we get an idea of what our attitude toward God should be. Because everything we have and are and ever will be is possible because of grace, we should approach God in humble thanksgiving.

- Hear the Pharisee saying, "O God, I thank you that I am not like the rest of humanity." Does this attitude resonate in you? To which people or groups of people do you believe you are superior?

- Spend some time with the publican's prayer "O God, be merciful to me, a sinner." Repeat this prayer again and again as you breathe slowly. Let the words draw you to God's mercy.

Fourth Week
in Lent

Monday
Psalm 30:2,4-6,11-13
John 4:43-54
(The official's son is healed)

The royal official in this reading is a Gentile, a non-Jew, but his belief that Jesus can heal his sick boy transcends all racial and credal boundaries. This is the kind of simple faith to which we are called.

- Picture in your imagination the scene between Jesus and the official. Hear the man continue pleading, despite Jesus' objections. See Jesus' face as he recognizes the great faith the official has in him.

- Rise from your prayer position and begin walking slowly around the room. With each step you take, believe that God will grant you the strength to persevere in love through any problems you might be having now. After awhile, relax again and give thanks to God for the gift of faith.

Tuesday
Psalm 46:2-3,5-6,8-9
John 5:1-3,5-16
(A healing in Jerusalem)

Jesus found people suffering and abandoned everywhere. In today's reading he notes the faith and hope of a man who has been suffering for thirty-eight years. Jesus heals him but is criticized for doing so because it is the Sabbath, a day when such works are forbidden.

- What "moving waters" are you awaiting so that you can get about the business of living fully? How is this affecting you now?

- Hear Jesus saying to you, "Rise, take up your mat, and walk."

Wednesday
Psalm 145:8-9,13-14,17-18
John 5:17-30
(Jesus' credentials)

When the Jews criticize Jesus for healing on the Sabbath, he replies that his Father, who goes on working always, is not bound by Sabbath restrictions. He then invites the Jews to recognize the power at work in him as essential for life and death.

- Read this passage slowly, spending time with whatever verse catches your attention. Do not try to reflect on every phrase.

- Spend some time with the words "I do not seek my own will but the will of the one who sent me." Repeat them again and again as you allow your will to merge with God's.

Thursday
Psalm 106:19-23
John 5:31-47
(More on Jesus' credentials)

When Jesus claimed to be doing God's work, it was only natural that the Jews should ask him for proof that this was actually true. Crackpots and false messiahs abounded then, as now. Jesus points to the testimony of Moses and of John the Baptist, the Scriptures, and the works that he has done as evidence that his claims are not unfounded.

- What reasoning supports your faith in Jesus? How can you deepen your understanding of who Jesus is?

- What does human approval mean to you? How important is it in your involvement in the Church?

- Pray for the grace to be more detached from the need for human approval.

Friday
Psalm 34:17-21,23
John 7:1-2,10,25-30
(On Christ's origins)

The Jews had many preconceptions about from where the Messiah would come, what he would be like, and what he would do. Many of these preconceptions prevented them from recognizing Jesus as the one for whom they had prayed.

- Have you, like Jesus, ever been misjudged and limited by others who drew hasty conclusions about you? Is this happening on a regular basis even now? How are you handling it?

- What do you do to prevent your first impressions about other people from limiting your relationship with them?

- Pray for the grace to let God be God in your life.

Saturday
Psalm 7:2-3,9-12
John 7:40-53
(The people's response to Jesus)

It is obvious to many people that Jesus is an extraordinary man. Still they try to cast him in every role except the one which he himself proposes: God's Son.

- What do you think the temple guards experienced as they listened to Jesus? Have you ever experienced this? Get in touch with those memories and feelings.

- Make a commitment to do something special in the next week to help you draw closer to God.

Fifth Week
in Lent

Monday
Psalm 23:1-6
John 8:1-11
(Jesus and the adulterous woman)

Today's reading reveals depths of human malice which sicken Jesus. Having caught a woman (where was the man?) in the act of adultery, the authorities bring her to Jesus, attempting to pit his mercy against his justice and catch him in a trap. A pious tradition suggests that when Jesus traced in the dirt, he spelled out the sins of the self-righteous accusers, causing them to leave shamefaced.

- Imagine yourself as a bystander observing this scene between the authorities, Jesus, and the woman. Note the self-righteousness on the face of the authorities; watch Jesus writing on the ground and glancing up at each official in turn; see the gratitude in the woman's eyes; hear Jesus speaking words of forgiveness to her.

- Write your impressions from the imagination exercise. Note especially your impressions of Jesus.

Tuesday
Psalm 102:2-3,16-21
John 8:21-30
(Jesus is one with the Father)

Unlike Matthew, Mark, and Luke, John often has Jesus involved in long, profound dialogues with unbelievers and authorities. This is a method he uses to articulate his community's understanding of who Jesus is as they face persecution from Jews and Romans alike. In today's reading Jesus speaks of the revelation that is to come when he is lifted up, or crucified.

- Spend some time with the passage "The one who sent me is with me. He has not left me alone." Become aware of God's nearness and love for you.

- Make a resolution to let a special person in your life know that you care about him or her.

Wednesday
Daniel 3:52-56
John 8:31-42
(The meaning of freedom)

It is a paradox that untamed passions bring enslavement, whereas self-discipline brings freedom. Jesus promises that the discipline of living according to his teaching will bring freedom, for he is the Son who reveals to us the human way to God.

- What does freedom mean to you? What situations restrict your experience of freedom? What limits your exercise of freedom?

- Resolve to discipline a passion that has caused you to feel enslaved. Pray for the grace to have control over this passion.

Thursday
Psalm 105:4-9
John 8:51-59
(The eternal origin of the Christ)

The meeting of the human and divine in Jesus will be forever a mystery, an inexhaustible truth. Certainly the human Jesus was born of Mary in space and time. John, however, reminds us today that the great I AM (Yahweh), whose knowledge is of eternity, also lives in Jesus. The Jews consider such a belief blasphemous and attempt to stone Jesus.

- What does today's reading say to those who consider Jesus only a great man or one of several incarnations of God, along with Buddha and Mohammed, for example?

- Spend some time with the passage "If I glorify myself, my glory is worth nothing; but it is my Father who glorifies me." Write your impressions.

Friday
Psalm 18:2-7
John 10:31-42
(Jesus confronts his critics)

Before the Jews rush to hasty conclusions, Jesus again reminds them that his works confirm his words, and he invites them to reconsider their unfounded judgments against him. When they reply by trying to arrest him, he escapes because he is not yet ready to make his decisive confrontation.

- To whom do your works testify? To whom do you give the glory?

- Spend some time with the passage "The Father is in me and I am in the Father" and its equivalent in the First Letter of John: "The one who is in you is greater than the one who is in the world" (4:4). Pray for the grace to be filled with this power.

Saturday
Jeremiah 31:10-13
John 11:45-57
(Jesus is condemned to die)

This passage comes after the raising of Lazarus from the dead, an event which caused many Jews to put their faith in Jesus. The Sanhedrin was the great religious council, a gathering of prominent religious leaders similar to our own bishops' conference today. Caiaphas, the designated leader, proposes that killing Jesus is preferable to the destruction of the status quo. John turns this statement into a cryptic prophecy of Jesus' redemptive death and Resurrection.

- Leo Tolstoy wrote, "If, by doing God's will, I help to bring about the dissolution of the existing order of things, then the existing order of things needs to be changed." How does this statement differ from that of Caiaphas? Is there a middle ground between the two upon which a Christian can stand in good faith?

- Do you believe that any of the civil laws of your government conflict with the values of Christ? What stand do you take in such a conflict?

Holy Week

Monday
Psalm 27:1-3,13-14
John 12:1-11
(Mary anoints Jesus)

We begin Holy Week with a reading that anticipates Jesus' death and burial. Earlier in John's Gospel, Mary had chosen to sit at the feet of Jesus while
Martha, her sister, criticized her for not helping with
housework. In today's passage Judas criticizes Mary
for her extravagant expression of love for Jesus, but
Jesus rebukes him and affirms her display as pro-
phetic of his burial.

- Do you believe that money and time spent on
  Christian art and on church worship space are
  scandalous in a world where so many are poor?

- Resolve to demonstrate your love for another
  person in an extravagant way for the glory of
  God.

Tuesday
Psalm 71:1-6,15,17
John 13:21-33,36-38
(Judas betrays Jesus)

It is very likely that Judas was a man with many
admirable qualities; otherwise Jesus would not have
chosen him to be an apostle. Judas did not like the
way things were turning out, however, and probably hoped that the confrontation he was forcing
between Jesus and the authorities would put some
sense into Jesus. Judas' plan backfired, as we know,

but Jesus views this betrayal as the beginning of his hour of glory.

- What are some of the ways in which you betray Jesus? Make a list and pray for forgiveness.

- Spend some time with the passage "Where I am going, you cannot follow me now, though you will follow later."

Wednesday
Psalm 69:8-10,21-22,31,33-34
Matthew 26:14-25
(The Passover meal begins)

The Passover was a Jewish feast recalling the historical Exodus of the Jews and their liberation from Egyptian domination and persecution. Jesus, a Jew, deeply loved this tradition and chose to share it with his most intimate friends, the apostles. This particular Passover meal will take on a new meaning in the light of the crucifixion and Resurrection of Jesus.

- How important to you is the sharing of a meal with friends and/or family? How does the sharing of a meal help to build relationships?

- Look into the possibility of sharing a Passover meal with a church group or community.

Holy Thursday
Psalm 116:12-13,15-18
John 13:1-15
(Jesus washes the apostles' feet)

This is Jesus' final evening with his apostles. He begins to say farewell and prepares for the treachery to come. Matthew, Mark, and Luke emphasize the sharing of the bread and wine, with Jesus asking the apostles to remember him in that manner. John, however, shows Jesus washing the apostles' feet as the last symbolic intimacy he will share with them.

- Bishop Sheen once wrote that, although we have Jesus' example of the washing of the apostles' feet as a model of service, it is difficult to find people today fighting for the towel. Is this true of you? What are some of the lowly jobs at home and at work you avoid because you feel they are beneath your dignity?

- Pray for the grace to be washed clean of false pride.

Good Friday
Psalm 31:2,6,12-13,15-17,25
John 18:1-19:42
(Jesus arrested, condemned, crucified)

Crucifixion was not the kind of death a community would choose for its hero. Roman crucifixion was reserved for the most heinous criminals in society and was intended to discourage other criminals from testing the Pax Romana. Since the Jews were not permitted to carry out the death sentence, they needed to convince the Roman procurator, Pontius Pilate, that Jesus deserved to die. Though Pilate seems reluctant to comply, he finally gives in, and Jesus is "lifted up."

- After reading through John's passion narrative, spend some time reflecting on the cost of loving as Jesus loved.

- Bonhoeffer, a Protestant pastor killed by the Nazis, wrote that when Jesus Christ calls a person, he bids him or her to come and die. How do you feel about this?

- Pray for the grace to be willing to lay down your life today for the sake of love.

The Season of Easter

Easter is the day of Christ's victory over sin and death. Baptism initiates us into fellowship with Jesus and gives us the right to stand before God and plead for the graces won by him. During the season of Easter, we will consider the implications of being an Easter people—a people who live in full confidence that power will be given us to live a life free from the shackles of shame, fear, and despair.

First Week of Easter

Monday
Psalm 16:1-2,5,7-11
Matthew 28:8-15
(Jesus appears to the women)

In Matthew's Resurrection narrative, Jesus appears first to women, commissioning them to go to the apostles. They are the first evangelists to bring the Good News of the Resurrection to the world—an awesome elevation of the role of women in a male-dominated culture. The story that Jesus' body had been stolen by his disciples reminds us that belief in the Resurrection was disputed by some even from the beginning.

- Do you believe Jesus of Nazareth was raised from the dead? Do you believe that you, too, will be— and are even now being—raised to new life? What does that mean to you?

- How can you communicate the joy of Easter to those with whom you will be interacting today?

Tuesday
Psalm 33:4-5,18-20,22
John 20:11-18
(Jesus appears to Mary of Magdala)

Mary of Magdala was judged harshly by society, yet she was one of the few who followed Jesus to the cross. In today's reading Jesus appears to her, commissioning her to tell his disciples that he is risen.

Those who love deeply are those who will see Christ, as Mary discovers.

- In your imagination, accompany Mary, feeling the depths of her grief as she approaches the tomb only to discover that Jesus' corpse is gone. Experience her longing for Jesus as she pleads with him (the gardener) to tell him where she can find the corpse and get it back. Rejoice with her when Jesus calls her name. Adore Jesus with her as she embraces him.

- Pray for the grace to believe that Jesus is truly risen.

Wednesday
Psalm 105:1-4,6-9
Luke 24:13-35
(The road to Emmaus)

Those who loved Jesus were crushed by his scandalous death. Whatever he had promised them concerning his Resurrection must have been poorly understood, because his followers were deeply shaken when they learned that his tomb was empty. The disciples' experience on the road to Emmaus gives us an idea of how their sorrow was turned to joy.

- Imagine yourself walking down a lonely road with Jesus by your side. Pour out your heart to him; tell him everything that has been weighing heavily upon you. Write in your journal the response you believe he is giving you.

- What is the significance of the verses concerning the breaking of the bread? How important to you is breaking bread with other Christians?

Thursday
Psalm 8:2,5-9
Luke 24:35-48
(Jesus appears to his disciples)

There is little doubt that Jesus' disciples believed that he had been raised from the dead and that they experienced him in a profoundly significant way. In today's reading Luke tries to express some of the impressions left by the risen Christ on his disciples. He leaves us with as many questions as answers, however. What was the nature of this risen body, for example? These are questions we cannot answer. Like the disciples, we are simply invited to accept Jesus as our risen lord.

- How do you feel about the prospect of your own death? How does belief in the Resurrection help you live more fully before death?

- Spend some time hearing Jesus say to you, "Peace be with you."

Friday
Psalm 118:1-2,4,22-27
John 21:1-14
(Appearance by the Sea of Tiberius)

This passage is reminiscent of the call of Simon, Andrew, James, and John. Before Jesus called them to be disciples, they had been fishermen. Finding them fishing in the sea, the risen Jesus tells them to cast out one more time; they net an abundance of fish. Jesus then nourishes them for their new role as fishers of people.

- How does God's grace nourish you in your daily work? Do you believe your work and the successes you've had are entirely because of your own efforts or because grace has helped you get where you are?

- Do you consider yourself a fisher of people? What does this mean to you?

- Pray for the grace to recognize God working in your life.

Saturday
Psalm 118: 1,14-21
Mark 16:9-15
(Appearances to the faithful)

Mark's account seems to summarize the appearances we have reflected upon this week. Unlike the other passages, however, we observe Jesus reproaching the apostles for their unwillingness to believe what they had heard from Mary and the disciples who had returned from Emmaus. The Good News comes to us from the words of these first evangelists and we, too, are invited to believe their words.

- The Resurrection of Jesus can neither be proved nor disproved. Rather, we are invited to believe the testimony of those who experienced him and then shared this experience with others. How do you feel about this dynamic? Is it easy for you to believe the word of others?

- What experience or information would make it easier for you to believe in the Resurrection?

Second Week
of Easter

Monday
Psalm 2:1-9
John 3:1-8
(Jesus and Nicodemus)

The dialogue between Jesus and Nicodemus gives us some ideas about the new life that comes to us through the risen Christ. Nicodemus has come at night because he fears the Jews; he expresses a very tentative faith in Jesus. Jesus responds by inviting Nicodemus to experience a renewed identity through baptism and the Holy Spirit.

- What does the phrase "born of the Spirit" mean to you? Do you consider yourself born of the Spirit?

- What keeps you from completely giving your life over to Jesus?

Tuesday
Psalm 93:1-2,5
John 3:7-15
(Jesus the revealer of God)

In today's reading John proposes that we accept Jesus as the one who reveals to us what we need to know about God. Human reason is confined to knowledge of this world, Jesus tells Nicodemus. Knowledge of God must come from one who is of God. Faith in Jesus lets us share in this knowledge.

- Do you believe that the truths of divine revelation conflict in any way with what human reason can demonstrate to be true? If so, what are you doing to clarify your thinking?

- What did Jesus reveal to us about God that is most important to you? Spend some time thanking God for this gift.

Wednesday
Psalm 34:2-9
John 3:16-21
(Jesus sent to save, not judge)

Many people believe that God's judgment works as a positive endorsement for, or negative decision against, us. Jesus' teaching about light and darkness reminds us that judgment means that God will honor the choices we have freely made. Those who reject Jesus and the way to God, he reveals, will be allowed to experience the darkness of soul they have chosen. God gives us freedom to respond to his love or to reject him. If this were not true, we could not share in God's love.

- Verse 20 implies that those who hate the light are ashamed and afraid to change. Is there anything from your past of which you are ashamed and believe that God has not forgiven? Ask for forgiveness.

- Is it easy for you to change attitudes and behaviors that conflict with the way of love? Pray for the grace to change.

Thursday
Psalm 34:2,9,17-20
John 3:31-36
(Jesus is Lord of all)

John unhesitantly proclaims that Jesus is formed from above, meaning Jesus is God. He does not see Jesus as merely an enlightened or wise man or a prophet. Rather, Jesus is one who speaks God's own words, and our response to him should be one of reverent obedience.

- Many saints have said that obedience to Jesus allowed them to fully experience freedom. Do you experience the truth of this paradox in your own life?

- In what area of your life are you most obedient to Jesus? Most disobedient?

- Pray for the grace to allow Jesus to be Lord of your life.

Friday
Psalm 27:1,4,13-14
John 6:1-15
(Miracle of the loaves)

This account of the feeding of the multitude is common to all four gospels and represents one of the most enduring and significant traditions. Most theologians see in this miracle a connection with the belief in Jesus as the Bread of Life who satisfies all our hungers.

- Jesus blessed the little that was offered in a spirit of sharing. Do you believe that your gifts of time, talent, and money offered in love are blessed by God? How do you experience this blessing?

- What can you offer to share with others today in a spirit of love? Ask God to bless your offering.

Saturday
Psalm 33:1-2,4-5,18-19
John 6:16-21
(Jesus walks on water)

Today's reading is yet another example of an incident presented by the evangelist to appeal to faith and not to invite skepticism. The meaning of Jesus' walk on the water is that he rejoined his disciples. It reminds us that nothing can separate us from the love of the risen Christ.

- What are the primary causes of stress and anxiety in your life? What lifestyle changes can you make to eliminate some of the more destructive causes of stress?

- Let your imagination create a sea filled with your usual sources of stress and needless anxiety. Invite Jesus to walk over these troubled waters in your mind. Hear him saying, "It is I. Do not be afraid."

Third Week of Easter

Monday
Psalm 119:23-24,26-27,29-30
John 6:22-29
(The people seek their king)

Jesus had fed the crowds, and they were eager to make him king. Knowing this, he fled from their midst and joined his disciples in their boat. Now the crowd searches for him, for anyone who can feed multitudes by blessing a few crumbs can solve all logistical problems involved in making war against the Romans. Jesus corrects their misconception about him by inviting them to work for the kind of food that will last.

- Are you looking for Jesus? Where? How do you think you can find him?
- Pray for the grace to hunger for the things of God.

Tuesday
Psalm 31:3-4,6-8,17,21
John 6:30-35
(Jesus, the Bread of Life)

One way the evangelists tried to convert Jews was by explaining how Jesus fulfilled the prophecies of their ancestors. In today's reading John shows Jesus explaining that the manna which the Jews ate in the desert was only a symbol for the Bread which satisfies all hungers.

- What actions of yours are signs to others that you are a follower of Jesus Christ?
- Spend some time letting God love you and satisfy your spiritual hungers.

Wednesday
Psalm 66:1-7
John 6:35-40
(We shall be raised up)

Today's reading teaches us a tremendous lesson. Jesus' Resurrection demonstrated the power of God over the forces of evil and guaranteed that those who are with Jesus shall themselves be raised up. This shall be true for us as long as we strive to do the will of the one who has sent Jesus.

- Grace refers to all those unearned blessings that help make us who we are. Reflect on some of the graces from your early life and family that have helped form you (parents, teachers, place of birth, for example). List these in your journal and give thanks to God for them.
- Spend some time with the passage "I have come not to do my own will, but the will of him who sent me."

Thursday
Psalm 66:8-9,16-17,20
John 6:44-51
(Jesus, the Living Bread)

The Jews had complained that Jesus could not be from God since they knew of his human origins. Jesus now replies that there is a spiritual side to him that is of God. If they want to know about God, they need only to look to him.

- What are some of the sources of grace in your life now? How do these gifts help to make you who you are?

- Think of some way to let the people who are grace to you know that you are thankful for the gifts they bring to your life.

Friday
Psalm 117:1-2
John 6:52-59
(More on the Bread of Life)

These are some of the most uncompromising words ever attributed to Jesus. The Greek word for flesh used by John refers to bodily flesh, causing us to ask, with the Jews, "How can this man give us (his) flesh to eat?" This unmistakable allusion to the importance of the Eucharist should remind us that Jesus' gift of his life is the greatest gift we can receive.

- Many people who proclaim Jesus as their lord and savior speak of him as having died for their sins. How do you understand this? How has Jesus given his life for you?

- List a few of the many changes that have come to the world because of Jesus. Spend some time thanking God for these graces which determine the social and cultural contexts of our lives.

Saturday
Psalm 116:12-17
John 6:60-69
(Spirit and life)

John concludes his reflection on the Bread of Life by pointing out that the most important aspect of Jesus' teaching is that it reveals to us what is spirit and life. Many of Jesus' followers can not accept his teachings, and so they leave him. When confronted with this choice, the apostles, with Peter as their spokesman, proclaim their faith in Jesus.

- What teaching about Jesus (or other Church teaching) do you find hard to accept? What are you doing to help clarify your understanding of this doctrine?

- Many people forsake Jesus and his way every day. Hear him asking you, "Do you want to leave me too?" Give him your response.

Fourth Week of Easter

Monday
Psalm 42:2-3;43:3-4
John 10:1-10
(The Good Shepherd)

Jesus used many examples to explain the relationship between God and people. In today's reading John recalls Jesus identifying himself as the sheepgate. Out in the fields, sheep were herded into corrals. Shepherds slept in the openings of the corrals to protect the sheep. So, too, has Jesus laid down his life for us.

- Do you believe that following Jesus will enable you to experience life to the fullest? What is the full life?

- Spend some time reflecting on Jesus' promise to be committed to our growth and development. How does this make you feel?

Tuesday
Psalm 87:1-7
John 10:22-30
(Jesus is one with the Father)

Today's reading brings to mind a saying of C. S. Lewis who maintained that a man who said and did the things Jesus said and did was either who he said he was or else he was a lunatic on the level of a poached egg. There is no middle ground left to the interpreter of the meaning of Jesus' life;

Jesus does not intend that there be a middle ground.

- Who are the "sheep" whose well-being the Father has entrusted to you? Have you been faithful to them lately? How can you better love them?

- Pray for the grace to be more loving toward family members.

Wednesday
Psalm 67:2-3,5,6,8
John 12:44-50
(Jesus' word shall judge)

The Resurrection signified that God had set his seal on Jesus, that his claims are true, and that his teachings are authoritative. When confronted with the words of Jesus, our response becomes our judgment, for to refuse to live according to his way is to cut ourselves off from the fullness of life which he offers. Yet if we choose to accept him, we shall experience eternal life—life with God.

- How do you feel about non-Christians? Do you believe they can attain salvation? Do you feel any special obligation to enlighten them?

- Pray for those people in your life who need to know Jesus in a more personal way.

Thursday
Psalm 89:2-3,21-22,25,27
John 13:16-20
(Jesus, the servant)

Jesus' Resurrection won for us the grace to love as God loves. This love is to take the form of loving service, however, and is not to be used for self-glorification.

- Leo Tolstoy wrote that people who live according to principles other than love can justify all sorts of treachery against other people, invoking their principles as a rationale. Do you believe this?

- Who are the primary beneficiaries of the loving service you offer? Can you expand this circle?

Friday
Psalm 2:6-11
John 14:1-6
(Jesus is the way, the truth, the life)

In today's reading Christian beliefs concerning Jesus are focused beautifully by John. Jesus is the firstborn of the new creation and he has gone to prepare a place for us. He has revealed to us the way, the truth, and the life that will unite us with him and with one another.

- Meditate on several words/phrases that express your understanding/experience of Jesus as the way, the truth, and the life.

- Does your belief in life after death empower you to live more fully now, or does it cause you to procrastinate your life away?

Saturday
Psalm 98:1-4
John 14:7-14
(The great works to come)

During his earthly ministry, Jesus offered many inspiring examples of the Father's care for us. Freed from the constraints of space and time, the risen

Jesus can now continue his ministry of building the kingdom of God through each of us. For the grace to help build this kingdom of love and justice, we need only ask.

- Who are the people who minister to your needs on a regular basis? Thank God for them, for they are grace in your life. Think of a creative way to let them know you appreciate them.

- Do you believe that God answers prayer? For what is it appropriate to ask? What does God really want to give us?

- Spend some time with the verse "Whoever has seen me has seen the Father." How true is this of you, your identity, and your works?

Fifth Week
of Easter

Monday
Psalm 115:1-4,15-16
John 14:21-26
(God dwells within us)

Today's reading reminds us that much about us is a mystery. We can never fully understand ourselves, for there are depths in each of us that only God can plumb. God alone knows the truth about us, so we should be slow to judge ourselves or, worse, to take a false pride in ourselves and our accomplishments.

- How do you understand the verse "I will love him and reveal myself to him"? How does God reveal himself to you?

- Do you believe that you know yourself? Do you have a sense of mystery about yourself?

- Spend time thanking God for the miracle that you are.

Tuesday
Psalm 145:10-13,21
John 14:27-31
(His peace he leaves us)

The kind of peace Jesus promises is *shalom*, which means "the fullness of life." Although many philosophies and value systems promise this kind of peace, Jesus alone seems able to help us experience it consistently.

- Would you describe your usual state of mind as one of peace? Why? Why not? What situations rob you of peace? When do you usually feel most at peace?

- Pray for the grace to accept the peace which Christ promised.

Wednesday
Psalm 122:1-5
John 15:1-8
(Jesus, the true vine)

The parable of the vine and the vinegrower expresses the nature of our relationship with God and with one another. Like branches, we are dependent on the vine for life and nourishment. If we are not pruned or disciplined, we shall squander our lives, just as unpruned vines do.

- Do you really believe that without God you can do nothing meaningful?

- How do you experience the trimming and pruning described in the parable? Does this help you to grow?

- Spend time thanking God for the growth you are experiencing at this time in your life.

Thursday
Psalm 96:1-3,10
John 15:9-11
(Jesus completes our joy)

In today's reading John explains the reason why Jesus came: he invites us to share in God's own joy. There is always something a bit hollow and transient in even our most intense experiences of human pleasure and happiness. Living in love as Christ invites us to live will increase our human joys and complete them.

- Spend some time with the verse "As the Father loves me, so I also love you."

- Would you describe yourself as a joyful person? Do you know any joyful people? Why are they joyful?

- Pray for the grace to be open to joy.

Friday
Psalm 57:8-12
John 15:12-17
(Love one another)

Thousands of pages of reflection have been written about Jesus Christ and the meaning of his revelation for us. Jesus sums up everything in today's reading, briefly and succinctly! We are to bear fruit for the glory of God, for God has chosen us to share with one another his love for us.

- A pious tradition suggests that at the end of our lives, when we stand before God, he will ask us only one question: "Have you lived your life in such a way as to show others that I loved you?" Using this past week as the basis for your answer, how will you respond?

- Do you believe that God has chosen you to be one of his friends? How do you experience this?

Saturday
Psalm 100:1-3,5
John 15:8-21
(The persecutions to come)

Jesus does not delude his followers with promises of a pain-free, "pie-in-the-sky" life. He experienced resistance and constant attack during his earthly ministry, and he warns us that we should not expect better treatment from those in darkness.

- Faulkner wrote that if he had to choose between experiencing pain and experiencing nothing, he would always choose pain. Would you? How does your attempt to follow Jesus cause you pain?

- Pray for the grace to find meaning in your experiences of pain.

Sixth Week
of Easter

Monday
Psalm 149:1-6,9
John 15:26-16:4
(We must bear witness)

With the Resurrection came a mandate: we are to spread the news of the forgiveness of sin and the victory over death which Jesus brought. To help us in this endeavor, God's own Spirit—the Spirit who raised Jesus from the dead—will be our helper.

- How do you feel about sharing your religious beliefs with family members? With friends? With working acquaintances?

- What are some key issues facing your local secular community? How involved are you in working through these issues?

- Pray to be filled with the Holy Spirit. (Do this with family and/or friends, if possible.)

Tuesday
Psalm 138:1-3,7-8
John 16:5-11
(The promise of the Spirit)

In some wonderful and mysterious way, Jesus' life, death, and resurrection enable us to enjoy a fuller relationship with God than was possible prior to his coming. John emphasizes this point today when Jesus tells his disciples that his going will be for their own good.

- Eugene Kennedy wrote that we do not become truly human until we grow close enough to others to be missed. This is what the disciples of Jesus felt when he bade them farewell. Do you enjoy this kind of closeness with anyone? Would anyone miss you if you were to die?

- Pray for the well-being of those special people in your life.

Wednesday
Psalm 148:1-2,11-14
John 16:12-15
(The Spirit will guide us)

The Church's understanding of the meaning of Jesus has grown considerably since John wrote his gospel, even though new truths concerning Jesus have not been revealed. Today's reading also hints at the unity of truth in the Spirit who leads us to all truth, religious and otherwise.

- What are you doing to further the development of your mind? Your knowledge of the Scriptures? How is this helpful to you?

- What kind of knowledge scares you? Why?

- Pray for the grace to find God in all truth.

Thursday • Ascension

Friday
Psalm 47:2-7
John 16:20-23
(Our hearts will rejoice)

The disciples of Jesus loved him dearly and were upset to hear him speak of leaving them. Jesus compares their sorrow to that of a woman in labor, suffering now but rejoicing when her child is born. So shall it be with those who long for the things of God.

• Gibran wrote, "Your joy is your sorrow unmasked....The deeper that sorrow carves into your being, the more joy you can contain." Has this been your experience?

• Who or what has brought you your greatest joys? What sorrows have accompanied these experiences?

Saturday
Psalm 47:2-3,8-10
John 16:23-28
(Ask, and you shall receive)

Many times in Scripture we read about asking or speaking in someone's name. In Jewish culture, this was tantamount to invoking the authority of the person whose name was being used to influence the person to whom one was speaking. When Jesus urges us to plead with the Father for things we need in his (Jesus') name, he is telling us that we, too, may now enjoy the same graces from God that he experienced. This is joyful news.

• How do you feel about asking for favors from God? Why?

• Is it easy for you to articulate your needs to others? What needs do you find most difficult to request help in fulfilling? Why?

• Pray for the grace to accept your limitations.

Seventh Week of Easter

Monday
Psalm 68:2-7
John 16:29-33
(The apostles' desertion prophesied)

Many times Jesus' disciples struggled to comprehend the meaning of his words. When, at the Last Supper, they believe that they finally understand him, Jesus sees through the shallowness of their comprehension. Faith in him without acceptance of the suffering that will accompany faith has been a problem for Christians from the beginning.

- What are some of the more urgent issues facing the Christian community to which you belong? How are you struggling to help work through these issues?

- Spend some time with the verse "I have told you this so that you might have peace in me." Allow that peace to pervade your being.

Tuesday
Psalm 68:10-11,20-21
John 17:1-11
(Jesus prays to the Father)

During the next few days we will reflect on the long, beautiful prayer of Jesus as he anticipates his hour of passion and glory. Through this prayer, John continues to teach us the nature of the relationship between Jesus, the Father, and humanity.

- How is Christ glorified in humanity? How is he glorified in your life?

- The goal of Ignatius of Loyola was to do all for the greater honor and glory of God. What do you think of this goal? Is this your goal?

Wednesday
Psalm 68:29-30,33-36
John 17:11-19
(Jesus consecrated for us)

The work of love is to unify people in a dynamic relationship of growth and development. In today's reading Jesus prays that we will be united with the Father in truth, and he offers the gift of his life to make this unity possible. This is the supreme act of love.

- How does the world hate you because of your fidelity to God's commandments? What do you think Jesus means by this?

- Hear the words of the psalmist describing the love of God, "I have loved you with [an everlasting] love; so I have kept my mercy toward you" (Jeremiah 31:3). Bask in the mystery of this great love.

Thursday
Psalm 16:1-2,5,7-11
John 17:20-26
(Jesus prays for us)

We often forget that Jesus is as concerned about our own walk in faith as he was for his disciples. By writing about this prayer of petition Jesus made on our behalf, John reminds us that Jesus continues to intercede for us before the Father.

- An old saying proclaims that our problem is not that we are not good, but that we settle for less than the best. Do you believe this? Are you striving to become the best person you can be? Are you satisfied with your present level of spiritual growth?

- Pray for the grace to appreciate God's commitment to loving you.

Friday
Psalm 103:1-2,11-12,19-20
John 21:15-19
(We now live for God)

Peter had denied Jesus three times and Jesus knew Peter must have felt terrible about this. That is why Jesus now gives Peter an opportunity to affirm his love by asking his disciple three times, "Do you love me?" With Peter's affirmative responses, Jesus states that acceptance of his love should move us to share our lives with others.

- How does God "put a belt around you and take you where you would rather not go"? What kind of person would you be if you were not committed to following Jesus Christ?

- Hear Jesus asking you, "Do you love me?" After a few minutes, give him your response.

Saturday
Psalm 11:4-5,7
John 21:20-25
(Jesus and John)

Tradition says that John was the only apostle to escape martyrdom. The conversation in today's reading between Jesus and Peter may represent an attempt by the evangelist or his own disciples to correct a belief among the early Christians that John would not die. The final sentence in this passage reminds us that the Scriptures are not historical documents in the modern sense, but are, instead, the early communities' faith-filled recollections of the meaning of Jesus' life, death, and resurrection.

- Are you ever envious of those who seem to have it better than you? Hear Jesus saying, "What concern of it is yours (what they have)? You are to follow me."

- Pray for the grace to "mind your own business" in following Jesus, to quit comparing yourself to others.

Ordinary Time
After Pentecost

Once again we turn our attention to the "ordinary" ministry of Jesus. This phase of Ordinary Time is the last—and longest—of the Church's liturgical seasons.

Ninth Week in Ordinary Time

Monday
Psalm 112:1-6
Mark 12:1-12
(Malice in the vineyard)

The parables of Jesus are symbolic statements about life, designed to hold a mirror before us so we might see who we are in God's sight. In today's reading Jesus describes Israel as a vineyard entrusted to its tenants, the religious leaders. These leaders kill or mistreat all who were sent to them by God, the owner of the vineyard. Still, Jesus promises, their wickedness will not prevail.

- What kind of steward are you for the people God has entrusted to you? For the environment? For the government?

- Sketch a Christ-cornerstone and lay additional stones representing your gifts on top of it, fashioning a building of some sort.

- Pray for the grace to become a good steward of creation.

Tuesday
Psalm 112:1-2,7-9
Mark 12:13-17
(God and Caesar)

Today's reading describes another important confrontation between Jesus and the authorities. They try to trap him by baiting him with tax resistance and secular alternatives, either of which will damage his influence. He sees through their maliciousness, however, and distinguishes between religious and secular responsibilities.

- Are you a good citizen? Do you participate in the political process at least by voting?

- Is it ever appropriate for a Christian to disobey governmental authorities? When?

Wednesday
Psalm 25:2-9
Mark 12:18-27
(The life to come)

The Sadducees were a small but powerful group of Jewish religious leaders. They rejected all traditions except those articulated in the Pentateuch, the first five books of the Bible, which give no hint of the immortal nature of the human spirit. Today's reading describes a trap set for Jesus by the Sadducees. Jesus tells them that their God is too small.

- What do you believe heaven is like? Is your idea of heaven merely an image of your own notions of Utopia?

- "Heaven begins on earth, or it does not begin at all," Louis Evely wrote. Do you believe this?

- Pray for the grace to love God above all things.

Thursday
Psalm 128:1-5
Mark 12:28-34
(The two great commandments)

The two great religious questions are: What kind of God is God? and What does God expect of human beings? Jesus answers these questions in today's reading by emphasizing the importance of love.

- Write a short statement about what it means to love God with all your heart, soul, mind, and strength. Do these reflections describe your love of God?

- Augustine maintained that loving and praising God is the greatest joy a human being can experience. Do you agree?

- Pray for the grace to love God more deeply.

Friday
Psalm 146:2,7-10
Mark 12:35-37
(David's Lord)

This is a difficult passage. Confronted by the Jews with numerous preconceptions as to what the Messiah would be like, Jesus tries to open their minds to new possibilities. The messiah will be far more than a blood descendant of David, Jesus assures them. He will be one whom even David would worship.

- What are some misconceptions you have about God that need to be changed? Perhaps the way you complete the following sentences will help you identify these notions.

  a. God can't love me; I'm too…

b. I can't know God; God is too…

c. I can't believe in Jesus; he's too…

- Pray for the grace to be more open to God's forgiveness and love for you.

Saturday
Tobit 13:2,6
Mark 12:38-44
(The widow's mite)

God will not judge us according to human standards but according to what we've done with what we've been given. In today's reading a poor widow is recognized by Jesus as an example of true generosity.

- Are you a generous person? Do you give more out of excess than want?

- It has often been said that Christian giving—of money, services, and talent, for example—ought to hurt the giver a little. Do you agree?

Tenth Week in Ordinary Time

Monday
Psalm 34:2-9
Matthew 5:1-12
(The Beatitudes)

As we begin our twelve weeks of reflection on the Gospel of Matthew, we hear the Beatitudes, a collection of promises extended to the lowly, the humble, and the just. "You are blest," Christ promises us. We need only claim our blessings.

- With which beatitude do you identify most closely? Which do you relate to least? Why?

- Spend some time thanking God for his blessings.

Tuesday
Psalm 119:129-133,135
Matthew 5:13-16
(Shining lights)

Jesus is the new Moses. In depicting Jesus as the one who fulfilled the promises and prophecies of the Old Testament, Matthew gathers the teachings of Jesus and presents them in what is now called the Sermon on the Mount. Just as Moses ascended the mountain and returned with life-giving teachings, so Jesus does.

- "If you don't love yourself, it will be difficult for you to love others" is an old saying. Do you agree?

- What do you like most about yourself? What do you like least? How do these dislikes keep your light under a bushel basket?

- Pray for the grace to love yourself as God loves you.

Wednesday
Psalm 99:5-9
Matthew 5:17-19
(Jesus and the Law)

Today's reading summarizes much of what the Gospel of Matthew is attempting to articulate: Jesus is the fulfillment of Jewish expectations. Matthew constantly affirms the value of Jewish tradition and portrays Jesus as one who loved, rather than despised, Judaism.

- How do we teach one another to respect (or despise) the laws of God? Are you a model of most of these laws to your family? To those with whom you work?

- Who are the models to whom you look for inspiration in living out your faith? Why do these people inspire you?

Thursday
Psalm 85:9-14
Matthew 5:20-26
(On anger and reconciliation)

Jesus looks deeper than human behavior to identify sources of goodness and sin. Behavior follows one's state of being, he teaches; actions are always preceded by thoughts about the actions. If we are to transform our angry selves, we must begin to think peaceful thoughts, and we must also reconcile with our enemies.

- C. S. Lewis wrote that the Nazis hated the Jews and so they mistreated them. After a while they hated the Jews because they mistreated them. Are there people in your life who suffer the same lot from you?

- What are some occasions of anger for you? What do you usually do with your anger? How can you change your attitude toward these occasions to lessen your anger?

- Pray for the grace to be more patient with other people.

Friday
Psalm 116:10-11,15-18
Matthew 5:27-32
(Sexual responsibility)

The reproductive instinct is one of the strongest of human passions and one of the most difficult to control. Jesus tells us that the key to responsible sexual expression lies in the way we think about people of the opposite gender. Do we allow ourselves to fantasize adulterous thoughts? If so, we are violating God's law which holds that responsible sexual expression should take place in the context of a committed relationship.

- How do you view people of the opposite gender? Is it difficult for you to be friends with them? Are many of them friends with you?

- How do you feel about Jesus' teaching on adultery?

Saturday
Psalm 103:1-4,8-12
Matthew 5:33-37
(Integrity and sincerity)

God's name was considered sacred to Jews; they were forbidden to speak this name except in reverence. Moses had taught that the name of God should never be spoken in vain, and now Jesus states that a simple Yes or No should suffice for occasions when people are prone to swear.

- Do you tend to exaggerate events or twist the truth from time to time to impress others?

- How do you feel about people who curse regularly? Is this a harmless habit, or does it attract stormy thoughts that lead to angry behavior?

- Spend some time reverencing the name of Yahweh, "I Am Who Am."

Eleventh Week in Ordinary Time

Monday
Psalm 98:1-4
Matthew 5:38-42
(Nonviolent resistance)

Today's reading addresses the issue of breaking the cycle of violence. Because violence begets violence, Jesus commands his followers to refuse to perpetuate this cycle. Nonviolent resistance, he believes, is the best way to convert the violent of this world.

- "An eye for an eye is making the world blind," Gandhi said. Do you agree? Do you believe Jesus commanded us to refuse to stand up to evil? How should a Christian respond to evil?

Tuesday
Psalm 146 2,5-9
Matthew 5:43-48
(Love your enemies)

Jesus' command to love our enemies is one of his most challenging teachings. Because all people are children of God, we should love them all—even those with whom we disagree. Then will new things happen in our lives and in our world.

- Is it possible to disagree with someone and still love that person? Think of a few people with whom you often disagree; how can you love them?

- Do you believe it is ever appropriate for a Christian to kill someone with whom he or she disagrees?

- Pray for the grace to be able to recognize all people as children of God.

Wednesday
Psalm 112:1-4,9
Matthew 6:1-6,16-18
(Purity of heart)

Motives are important, Jesus teaches. People who are motivated by others' opinions are sure to fall short of that single-hearted love of God to which Jesus calls us. External motivations regarding charity and prayer can especially frustrate spiritual growth.

- Why do you pray? How important to you is it that others know you pray?

- Think of something nice you can do for someone today without that person knowing that you did it.

Thursday
Psalm 111:1-4,7-8
Matthew 6:7-15
(The Lord's Prayer)

Today's reading emphasizes the importance of being sincere and honest with God. Because God is not impressed by the length of time that we pray, or how many words we say, or how much we promise to give him, Jesus shares with us a formula for prayer that plugs us into grace and forgiveness.

- With each verse of the Lord's Prayer, spend some time reflecting on how your own life is influenced by these words. Add your own reflections.

- What faults in other people bother you most? How are these faults evident in your own life? Ask God for forgiveness.

Friday
Psalm 34:2-7
Matthew 6:19-23
(Heavenly treasure)

Again we return to the issue of motives. The philosopher Durant wrote that we do not desire that which we find reasonable, but we find reasons for that which we desire. Ignatius of Loyola stated that our motives are directed toward either love or selfishness. We should check our motives often.

- What do you treasure most in this world? How does your heart serve this treasure?

- Look back over the key events of the past day. What were your motives for saying and doing what you did?

- Pray for the grace to be motivated by love.

Saturday
Psalm 34:8-13
Matthew 6:24-34
(Trust in God)

This is one of the most cherished of Jesus' teachings. For those who treasure God's will above all else, he promises freedom from worry and peace of mind.

- What or whom do you worry about most often? What can you do to lessen your worries? How can you let go of unreasonable causes of worry?

- Because worry is usually directed toward future events over which we have no control in the present, resolve to spend more time in the present moment today, beginning now. Whenever worry arises, direct your attention back to the present, the only moment that exists.

Twelfth Week
in Ordinary Time

Monday
Psalm 33:12-13,18-20,22
Matthew 7:1-5
(Do not judge)

Christianity is a religion that emphasizes full, deep, intimate relationships between people. Because our judgments against other people limit our relationships with them, Jesus tells us to suspend judgment until we are perfect. For most of us, that will take forever.

- An old proverb says, "Search for the perfect church, and if you find it, join it. But know that as soon as you join it, it will have ceased to be the perfect church." What do you hold against your church? Why?

- Which family members have you judged most harshly? Pray for the grace to forgive yourself and them, and resolve to start anew in your relationship with them.

Tuesday
Psalm 15:2-5
Matthew 7:6,12-14
(The narrow gate)

Today's reading includes three loosely related teachings. As we strive to walk the difficult path of love, we are warned that we should not profane sacred truths and rituals by sharing them with people who cannot receive them or are not ready to. This caution does not mean that we should become exclusive or elitist, however.

- What golden rule sums up your philosophy about relationships with other people? How does this differ from verse 12?

- With what kinds of people do you find it difficult to share your beliefs about Christianity? How do you relate to these people?

Wednesday
Psalm 105:1-9
Matthew 7:15-20
(By their fruits...)

Now we come to the criterion for discerning truth: Examine the "fruits." Where the fruits of self-indulgence abound in a person's life, be aware of hypocrisy or false teaching (Galatians 5:19-21). Where the fruits of the Spirit adorn a person's life, listen to what he or she has to say (Galatians 5:22-24).

- List some of the spiritual fruits that you believe family members/co-workers would say characterize you. List the spiritual fruits that you see in yourself.

- Do you know anyone whose life is characterized by the fruits of the Spirit? Resolve to spend more time with this person.

Thursday
Psalm 106:1-5
Matthew 7:21-29
(Build on Jesus)

We conclude our meditation on the teachings of Jesus by listening to him tell us he wants far more than holy words to characterize our lives. He challenges us to build on the cornerstone he laid by acting lovingly through the day, each day.

- "Love God, and do as you please," Augustine wrote. Do you agree with this statement? Why? Why not?

- What are people missing who do not build their lives on Christ? How is this costly for them?

- Pray for the grace to believe more deeply in Jesus.

Friday
Psalm 128:1-5
Matthew 8:1-4
(Jesus heals a leper)

In many accounts of Jesus' healings, we hear him cautioning those he cured to tell no one. The leper in today's reading is instructed to go to the priests so he may be released from his banishment from society. The injunction to tell no one else reveals Jesus' concern for the proper interpretation of his miracles.

- Do you accept your body, its strengths, and its limitations?

- How do you think other people view your physical appearance? How much does it matter to you what they think?

- Pray for the grace to be able to accept yourself as you are now.

Saturday
Luke 1:46-50,53-55
Matthew 8:5-17
(More healings)

In the passage describing the cure of the centurion's son, Jesus shows us that he will respond to faith wherever he finds it. Allowing himself to be touched by the pain of others, he offers them healing and wholeness, regardless of their age or creed.

- What are you doing to take care of your body, a temple of the Holy Spirit? Do you ever abuse your body? How can you take better care of it?

- How willing are you to let other people share their pain with you? How do you decide when it is appropriate to say No to them?

Thirteenth Week in Ordinary Time

Monday
Psalm 103:1-4,8-11
Matthew 8:18-22
(The cost of discipleship)

At first glance, Jesus seems to be very hard on those he has invited to follow him. This passage, coming after accounts of healing, reveals that Jesus does not want people like the scribe to follow him on the impulse of the moment without first considering the cost. The man who wants to wait until he buries his father is not yet ready to leave home.

- What habit or relationship to which you have been clinging keeps you from making necessary changes in your life? Do something today to begin to grow out of this death-dealing security.

- "Today is the first day of the rest of your life" is a familiar maxim. Spend some time thinking about your day. Resolve to live it fully.

Tuesday
Psalm 26:2-3,9-12
Matthew 8:23-27
(Jesus calms a storm)

On the Sea of Galilee storms arise suddenly and violently. Just as quickly, they move along, leaving calm waters behind. Most significant in today's reading is not a revelation of Jesus' power over nature but a promise that if we have faith, he can calm the storms in our own lives.

- What are some sources of stress that you encounter regularly? Why do these situations cause you stress? How can you change your attitude about these situations to diminish stress?

- Pray for the grace to be more adaptable in stressful situations.

Wednesday
Psalm 34:7-8,10-13
Matthew 8:28-34
(Demoniacs and swineherds)

This is another miracle that is most meaningful when interpreted symbolically. Jesus' expulsion of the demoniacs into the swineherd does not indicate his displeasure over raising hogs (as some have written). Rather, it reveals his high esteem for human life.

- If you were to suddenly inherit $1 million, how would you change your lifestyle? How important is economics in your list of priorities?

- The Gadarenes ordered Jesus out of their district because he was obviously bad for business. Do you believe Jesus is still expelled by business? How?

Thursday
Psalm 116:1-9
Matthew 9:1-8
(Jesus and the paralytic)

Today's reading makes little sense unless we realize that Jews believed sickness was a manifestation of the power of sin in the world. By offering the paralytic forgiveness and healing, Jesus reveals his power over the forces of sin.

- How does sin most often break into your life? Hear Jesus' words "Courage child, your sins are forgiven." Pray for the grace to accept God's forgiveness.

- Do you know someone who is sick, depressed, or overburdened who would appreciate some support from you?

Friday
Psalm 106:1-5
Matthew 9:9-13
(The call of Matthew)

Matthew never forgot that Jesus had called him out of his position of disrepute and oppression. Whenever he mentions himself, Matthew quickly adds that he was once a tax collector. So, too, do we need to recall how the Lord has lifted us up and helped us grow.

- "When we remember, we are remembered" is a pious saying. Do you take enough time to recall your roots? Resolve to call a friend or family member today as a way to help you appreciate your past. Browse through an old photo album during the week.

- Are you a self-righteous person? How is this manifested in your life?

- Pray for the grace to recognize grace in your life.

Saturday
Psalm 135:1-6
Matthew 9:14-17
(Jesus the bridegroom)

Jesus came to bring a spirit of freshness and vitality among us. But if we are to grow in the Spirit, we must change old, self-centered, or outmoded ways of thinking about ourselves and life. If we do not change, the new wine of the Spirit will not remain within us.

- Does the prospect of continuing to grow (change) in Christ frighten you? What are you most reluctant to change? Why?

- Do you believe that the Church is open to changing outmoded traditions? Why are some people bothered by this? How important is it to you that the Church can be open to change when necessary?

- Pray for the grace to be willing to change for the sake of Christ.

Fourteenth Week in Ordinary Time

Monday
Psalm 91:1-4,14-15
Matthew 9:18-26
(Two miraculous cures)

In today's reading Jesus restores a young girl to life and heals an elderly woman who had hemorrhaged for twelve years. In an age when women and children are disenfranchised in society, Jesus' treatment of women is quite revolutionary.

- What does our culture consider qualities of masculinity and femininity? How do these stereotypes limit male and female self-expression?

- How do you feel about the Church's treatment of male and female sexuality? Why?

- Pray for the grace to be more open to the gifts of others.

Tuesday
Psalm 17:1-3,6-8,15
Matthew 9:32-38
(The harvest is rich)

Matthew shows Jesus healing a mute who then begins to speak. In this same reading Jesus encourages us to share his desire that people become more willing to minister to one another. Let us begin anew today.

- Do you believe there is a crisis in the Church in the area of ministry? Why? Why not?

- Do you consider yourself to be a minister?

Wednesday
Psalm 33:2-3,10-11,18-19
Matthew 10:1-7
(Jesus commissions the Twelve)

An old proverb says it is much easier for ten people to do the work of ten than for one person to try to do the work of ten. In choosing and commissioning disciples, Jesus multiplies his influence many times. His Spirit continues to support us in this model of ministry.

- Do you feel your community supports you and your ministerial endeavors? Do you need more support? How could you receive it?

- As you preview the events planned for your day, hear Jesus saying, "The reign of God is at hand." Let these words deepen your anticipation to love this day.

Thursday
Psalm 105:16-21
Matthew 10:7-15
(The command to travel light)

Jesus sends his disciples out into the towns and countryside with a simple message and a powerful ministry. They are to prepare the people for his own visitation. The disciples are told that though this task is worthy of room and board, some will reject them. Thus it is for all who try to be ministers of the gospel.

- Do you do your share to help support people committed to full-time ministry in the Church? What can you contribute of your time, talent, and money?

- Spend some time with the passage "The gifts you have received return as gifts." What are some of your gifts? How do you share these with others? What happens to you when you cling to your giftedness?

Friday
Psalm 37:3-4,18-19,27-28,39-40
Matthew 10:16-23
(Persecutions to come)

Because the early Church experienced persecution from Jews and Gentiles, Jesus' warning in today's reading offered words of consolation and hope. Persecution is to be expected even from family members, Jesus explains, but the consolation of the Spirit will be given to those in need.

- Do you believe that people today would crucify Jesus if he were to come among us in person as he did years ago?

- How have you been persecuted for Christ's sake during the past week?

- Pray for the grace of endurance.

Saturday
Psalm 105:1-4,6-7
Matthew 10:24-33
(The value of endurance)

Today Matthew offers still more consolation to a persecuted Church. If people are so callous as to call the Lord of love Beelzebul, should we not also expect the same treatment, he asks us. We should not allow such people to contaminate our souls, however. Endurance will bring us to Jesus.

- What does it mean to you to acknowledge Jesus before other people? How are you doing this in your life?
- Complete this sentence and reflect on it: "I would never deny Jesus unless…"
- Pray for the grace to know that God is closer to you than your very breath.

Fifteenth Week
in Ordinary Time

Monday
Psalm 124:1-8
Matthew 10:34-11:1
(Take up your cross)

The key to appreciating Jesus' message is to realize that he calls us to become more deeply related to other people. We do this not because they need us but because we need them to be ourselves. Because our selfishness opposes relationships, we must take up the cross of dying to selfishness.

- How do you feel about the verse "I have come to bring not peace but the sword"? What does Jesus mean by this?

- Place yourself somewhere on a continuum of attitudes regarding strangers. Strangers are:

    God's Grace ——————————— Nuisances

- Are you content to stay where you are on this continuum?

- Pray for the grace to be open to the gifts that others bring.

Tuesday
Psalm 69:3,14,30-34
Matthew 11:20-24
(Woes to towns)

If we are waiting for a greater gift from God than Jesus, we shall have to wait forever. This is the message Matthew shares in today's reading. It is not that the people of Chorazin, Bethsaida, and Capernaum reject Jesus but that they fail to reform.

- Do you take your nationality for granted? Your faith? Jesus? Spend some time thanking God for these gifts.

- Call to mind someone close to you who has drifted away in intimacy recently. Resolve to do something to make this relationship closer.

Wednesday
Psalm 103:1-4,6-7
Matthew 11:25-27
(Good News for the simple)

Accepting the Good News of Jesus Christ is less a matter of intellectual sophistication and more a matter of faith. In today's reading, Jesus warns us of the danger of intellectual snobbery.

- How do you respond to people who say, "How can you believe all that religious stuff? There's no proof for any of it"?

- Pray for the grace to accept Jesus in simplicity of heart.

Thursday
Psalm 105:1,5,8-9,24-27
Matthew 11:28-30
(Burdens removed)

When we try to live life only out of the capital of our own resources, we will surely become burdened. Those who embrace Jesus' way are promised shared burdens and spiritual refreshment.

- What burdens do you need help shouldering? Tell Jesus about them, articulating your feelings about these burdens. Ask him to let you know he is with you. Resolve to share these feelings with a friend whom you trust.

- Spend some time with the verse "Come to me...." Feel God's desire for you.

Friday
Psalm 116:12-18
Matthew 12:1-8
(God wants mercy)

At this point in Matthew's Gospel, the Jewish authorities begin to openly try to trap Jesus and discredit his ministry. Jesus does not accept their accusations of disobedience to the Law, however, reminding them that the mercy of God is the heart of the Law.

- What are some key issues facing the Church today? What are you doing to inform yourself about these issues? How are you expressing your opinions about the Church?

- How do you generally react when other people confront you for something you've done wrong? Why do you respond like this? Is there a better way to respond?

Saturday
Psalm 136:1,23-24,10-15
Matthew 12:14-21
(Jesus as Isaiah's servant)

The prophet Isaiah had described a servant who would be gentle of spirit yet despised by humanity. Though this mysterious figure was not usually associated with the glorious, kingly messiah expected by the Jews, Matthew tells us today that because our Messiah suffered for us, we can now hope.

- People followed Jesus because he was kind to them and his kindness aroused affection in them. What do you seek more of from others: affection or admiration (less intimate than affection)? Why?

- Spend some time with the verse "Behold my servant whom I have chosen, my beloved in whom I delight." Let God delight in you.

Sixteenth Week
in Ordinary Time

Monday
Exodus 15:1-6
Matthew 12:38-42
(The sign of Jonah)

It is doubtful that Jesus could have worked any kind of sign to inspire loving faith in the hearts of those who persecuted him. People who sought truth and who were humble found in him all that they needed.

- Father John Powell wrote that to the people who said to Jesus, "Show us and we will believe," Jesus replied, "Believe, and I will show you." What kind of knowledge does faith make possible?

- What kind of sign of God's presence is needed most in today's world? How can you manifest this sign today?

Tuesday
Exodus 15:8-10,12,17
Matthew 12:46-50
(The family of Christ)

"Your children are not your children," Gibran wrote. "They are the sons and daughters of Life's longing for itself." In today's reading, Jesus affirms the primacy of the family of God over blood relations.

- Have you left the home of your youth emotionally as well as physically? Are you still living your life according to adolescent patterns?

- What kind of esteem do you seek from family members? How important is this to you? Why?

- Pray for the grace to see all people as children of God.

Wednesday
Psalm 78:18-19,23-28
Matthew 13:1-9
(Parable of the sower)

Jesus reveals to us a God intent on communicating his love and vision. Because Jesus wants to reach more than the intellectuals of his day, he tells parables, simple stories, to describe the kingdom of God. Today's parable of the sower and the seed is rich with meaning concerning social development as well as our spiritual growth.

- What sentiments have you expressed at home recently? Choose one or two people from home and count the number of times you have affirmed them during the past two days. How many times have you criticized them? Resolve to be more loving.

- Spend some time allowing God to work in the soil of your heart.

Thursday
Daniel 3:52-56
Matthew 13:10-17
(More on parables)

Although the parables are relatively simple stories, they are nevertheless rich in symbolism. To appreciate their meaning, we must allow them to confront our lives as a mirror reflects back to us our bodily image. The more time and effort we put into the struggle of meditating on the parables, the greater will be our reward.

- "In the spiritual life, if you're not progressing, you're regressing." Do you agree with this? Why? Why not? In what area of your life have you made progress recently?

- Pray for the grace to hunger for growth.

Friday
Psalm 19:8-11
Matthew 13:18-23
(A parable explained)

Jesus taught his disciples many things that he did not explain to the crowds. He wanted to be certain that his disciples understood his words because he knew that they would one day need to expound on them. In today's reading he explains the meaning of the parable of the sower, leaving its symbolism intact while developing its meaning.

- What kinds of seeds have you sowed at work recently? Choose a few people with whom you work and examine how you have related to them during the past two days. How often were you critical of them, at least silently? Resolve to be more affirming.

- What is growing in the good soil of your heart? In the briers? In the rocky ground? Along the path?

Saturday
Psalm 50:1-2,5-6,14-15
Matthew 13:24-30
(Parable of the weeds and wheat)

This parable is extremely rich in meaning. The weeds, known as darnel or bastard wheat in some translations, are almost impossible to distinguish from the wheat when both are seedlings. Because God is a wheat grower and not a weed puller, he allows both to grow together.

- "That which seems most feeble and bewildered in you is the strongest and most determined," Gibran wrote. What kind of strength is he talking about here?

- The converse of the above statement might be "That which you think is your greatest character asset is often your downfall." Have you ever experienced this?

Seventeenth Week in Ordinary Time

Monday
Psalm 106:19-23
Matthew 13:31-35
(Parables of growth)

"Things take time," proclaims a poster circulated widely today. Jesus would have concurred. Although beginning in relative obscurity, the influence of Christ through his Church has been a powerful leaven for good in the world. His influence in our lives can be no less encouraging.

- Are you a better person now than you were six months ago? One year ago? Five years ago? How?

- Spend some time with this passage from Paul's writings: "Although the outer self is wasting away, our inner self is being renewed day by day" (2 Corinthians 4:16).

Tuesday
Psalm 103:6-13
Matthew 13:35-43
(Parable of the weeds explained)

Again we find Jesus explaining his parables to his disciples, but he invites everyone to be open to his teaching. We live in a world that is both good and bad, Jesus tells us. God can purge the evil from our midst, but we must hear his words of love and put them into practice.

- Some philosophers have argued that goodness is

merely the absence of evil; others, notably Augustine, argued that evil is the absence of good. Where do you stand on the issue of sources of good and evil?

- How does hearing God's word help you to become a better person? Write down your thoughts. Spend some time thanking God for the gift of the Scriptures.

Wednesday
Psalm 99:5-7,9
Matthew 13:44-46
(The pearl of great price)

The two mini-parables in today's reading emphasize the kind of response to Jesus to which we are called. Like the people in the parables, we are invited to set his kingdom as our highest priority, organizing our lives according to God's will.

- If you could write a job description explicitly suited for your most complete response to Jesus, what would it include (type of work, salary, benefits, with whom you would work, for example)? How closely does your present occupation resemble this ideal work? How long do you intend to remain in your present occupation?

- Pray for the grace to treasure the things of God.

Thursday
Psalm 84:3-6,8,11
Matthew 13:47-53
(Parable of the dragnet)

Today's parable teaches us an important lesson. Jesus has come to transform humanity, but he also accepts the messiness of the world. So, too, are we invited to accept our messy world and broken lives as worthy of transformation.

• Imagine that God has cast a spiritual dragnet into your soul today. What would be dragged out? What would you most like to keep? What do you want to throw away?

• Pray for the grace to know that God loves you just as you are now.

Friday
Psalm 81:3-6,10-11
Matthew 13:54-58
(His own town rejects Jesus)

It is ironic that the people with whom we are the closest are also the people who often limit us most. This is what happened to Jesus in Nazareth. His brethren (relatives) are not open to his ministry because their ideas of him are too limited.

• Do you feel that the people with whom you live love and accept you the way you are? Do the people with whom you work love and accept you?

• "We like people in proportion to the good we do them and not in proportion to the good they do us," Laurence Sterne wrote. Do you agree?

Saturday
Psalm 67:2-3,5,7-8
Matthew 14:1-12
(John the Baptist beheaded)

The Navajo Indians believed that conscience was a tiny triangle that turned inside the human heart.

When a person tended toward immorality, the triangle rubbed the walls of the heart and caused pain, helping steer that person back toward goodness. When a person became so immoral that the points on the triangle were smoothed out, he or she felt nothing in conscience any longer.

- Do you believe that some people are hopelessly wicked?

- Do you believe you have a well-formed conscience? Are you sensitive to your conscience? How do you feel when you behave contrary to your conscience? What do you usually do with these feelings?

Eighteenth Week in Ordinary Time

Monday
Psalm 81:12-17
Matthew 14:13-21
(Jesus feeds the multitudes)

Jesus loved John the Baptist very deeply. When he hears of John's death, he seeks a lonely place where he can mourn the loss of his friend, but the crowds deny him even this small amount of privacy. His response to them is one of mercy, however, and not reproach.

- "My interruptions are my work," Henri Nouwen wrote. How do you handle interruptions? Do you believe that some interruptions are God's way of breaking into your life?

- Think over your day, anticipating times when you will probably be interrupted. How can you respond in a loving way? Pray for the grace to remember to do so when those times come.

Tuesday
Psalm 51:3-7,12-13
Matthew 14:22-36
(Jesus, the mysterious)

Today's reading includes many mysterious events ascribed to Jesus. After feeding a crowd with a miraculous meal, he sends the people back to their homes; he prays; he walks on the water; and he heals people who touch his clothing. There are many things about Jesus that Peter does not understand, but Jesus invites Peter to believe and to trust. Jesus invites us to do the same.

- What notions about Jesus make it difficult for you to believe and trust in him? From whom can you seek guidance in working through these blocks to personal growth? Resolve to do so during the coming week.

- Although he had a very busy schedule, Jesus nevertheless found time to pray. How faithful to prayer are you? How important to you is prayer?

Wednesday
Psalm 106:6-7,13-14,21-23
Matthew 15:21-28
(Messiah of the Gentiles)

This passage describes an event which took place during the only time Jesus ever ventured outside Jewish territory. While seeking respite from the demands of the crowds who followed him and from the authorities who tormented him, he is confronted by a persistent Canaanite woman. Even though she is a Gentile and, as a Canaanite, a member of the Jews' most ancient enemy, her faith and love finally move Jesus to grant her requests.

- "The family that prays together, stays together" is a familiar saying. How important is praying and worshipping as a family to you? Resolve to find books and pamphlets on family prayer to help deepen this experience.

- Spend some time thanking God for those people in your life who love you.

Thursday
Psalm 95:1-2,6-9
Matthew 16:13-23
(Jesus, Peter, and the Church)

Of the four evangelists, only Matthew speaks of Jesus founding the Church. He also speaks of the privileged place of Peter as leader of the Church—a responsibility so important that Peter's words would become binding for the salvation of souls. When Peter tries to sway Jesus from his destiny, Jesus rebukes him; as leader of the Church, Peter must learn to submit his will to God's.

- Spend some time with the passage "Who do you say that I am?" Respond as honestly as you can.

- How do you feel about the manner in which Church authorities exercise power? On what issues do you respect their leadership most? Least?

- Pray that our Church leaders may exercise authority wisely.

Friday
Psalm 77:12-16,21
Matthew 16:24-28
(The meaning of self-denial)

The gospel says we must die to ourselves, so it is important that we understand what this means. Jesus neither calls us to despise ourselves nor to deny our personal dreams and ambitions—unless they lead to sin. The self we are to deny is that strong tendency in each of us to be selfish and unconnected to others—to be ruled by instinct and desire rather than by truth and love. The cross is the way to grow into the higher, spiritual self.

- Review your past day, focusing on a few key events. What decisions did you make? What were your motives behind these decisions?

- "Incarnation happens with every decision to love" is a doctrine of the mystics. How do you understand this? Pray for the grace to be more conscious of the loving alternatives you have for each decision you make.

Saturday
Psalm 18:2-4,47,51
Matthew 17:14-20
(Jesus cures a young boy)

Jesus' actions among us reveal a God who views suffering and illness as tragedies. Rather than send misery into our lives, God wants to help us cope as we persist in our struggles. The key to such persistence is faith; we constantly need to pray for faith.

- How do you feel about the impatience shown by Jesus in today's reading? Does this make it easier for you to believe in him?

- Think of several ways you could complete this open-ended sentence: "If I had more faith, I could...." Examine your responses and ask God to grant you the faith you need to accomplish one of these dreams in the near future.

Nineteenth Week in Ordinary Time

Monday

Psalm 147:12-15,19-20
Matthew 17:22-27
(The temple tax)

Although Jesus has been careful to avoid proclaiming himself the Son of God, today's reading alludes to this claim. Because the Temple is considered God's house, he explains, he, the son of the King of creation, should not have to pay the temple tax. Only Matthew relates this story and the account of Peter's extracting the coin from a fish (perhaps an allusion to Peter's trade).

- How do you feel about cheating on income taxes?

- "God helps those who help themselves" is a popular saying. Do you believe this? Why? Why not?

Tuesday

Deuteronomy 32:3-4,7-9,12
Matthew 18:1-5,10,12-14
(Childlike faith)

Acknowledging our absolute dependence on grace is the first step toward spiritual growth. People who are self-important cut themselves off from grace. This is why Jesus holds out a little child as a model for us, assuring us that our standards of importance are not God's.

- In what ways are you aware of being dependent on God? Do you believe that you have accomplished anything without God's help?

- The parable of the lost sheep teaches us that God loves individuals, not just groups of people. Spend some time simply relaxing in the awareness that God loves *you*, knows *you*, and delights in *you*.

Wednesday
Psalm 66:1-3,5,8,16-17
Matthew 18:15-20
(Reconciliation process)

Because the kingdom of God is characterized by people living in deep, growing relationships, we must make every effort to be reconciled with one another when our differences separate us. If our individual efforts fail, then we should seek help. There may come a point beyond which we will find reconciliation impossible, but we should not be too hasty in drawing this conclusion.

- Which do you find easier: to attempt reconciliation with those from whom you are separated, or to remain angry and justified in your anger against them? How does each response affect your attitude toward others?

- How do you feel about praying with other people? What do verses 19-20 promise?

Thursday
Psalm 114:1-6
Matthew 18:21-19:1
(The mercy of God)

Forgiveness is one of the most humbling of all practices and one of the most difficult. That is why Peter asks Jesus if there is a limit to the number of times that God—and we—can forgive others. Jesus' reply reveals the incomprehensible depths of God's forgiveness and our awesome responsibility to extend this grace to others.

- Suppose God were to treat you as you have treated other people. How well would you fare? Which would you prefer to have God extend to you, justice or mercy?

- Is it difficult for you to forgive those who have wronged you? Is it difficult to ask for forgiveness when you've done wrong to another?

- Pray for the grace to know that you are a forgiven sinner.

Friday
Psalm 136:1-3,16-18,21-22,24
Matthew 19:3-12
(Marriage and divorce)

To understand the significance of today's reading, we must first realize that some Jewish traditions permitted a man to divorce his wife if he had lost interest in her or found her wanting in household skills. Jesus counters this tradition by holding out as God's will the indissolubility of the marriage commitment. He also states some people would be better off not married.

193

- Several early Fathers of the Church believed that God frowned on sexual intercourse and that the Holy Spirit deserted people during sexual union. What is your response to such an assertion?

- Why would an adult person *choose* to remain unmarried? Do you believe this is healthy?

Saturday
Psalm 16:1-2,5,7-8,11
Matthew 19:13-15
(Jesus and the children)

Jesus' kindness was shared with all, including the little and unimportant people in society. He saw the innocence and potential in children and loved them without reserve. Today's reading describes one of the most touching of all encounters between Jesus and people in the Bible.

- George Macdonald said that children should not be afraid of anyone who follows Jesus. Do you agree? How do you feel about children?

- How do you feel about abortion? Have you taken a stand to help people who are struggling with this issue?

Twentieth Week in Ordinary Time

Monday
Psalm 106:34-40,43-44
Matthew 19:16-22
(The rich young man)

This is a parable for today's people. Jesus tells the rich young man that it is not enough to keep the Law. Jesus challenged him to throw away false securities and become a disciple. Unfortunately, the young man found this invitation too difficult to accept.

- The philosopher Schopenhauer stated that life vacillates between suffering (the fate of the poor and broken) and boredom (the fate of the rich and secure). Do you agree?

- Paul stated that the love of money is the root of all evil. How much money do you need to support the lifestyle to which you believe Christ is calling you?

- Pray for the grace to be more attached to the things of God.

Tuesday
Psalm 85:9,11-14
Matthew 19:23-30
(Wealth and salvation)

Monetary wealth is attractive because it affords us numerous opportunities for entertainment, education, and influence unavailable to the poor. Thus money is a primary competitor with God for the hearts of people. In today's reading Jesus promises a wealth of experience to those who embrace his way.

- "The state of life is most happy where superfluities are not required and necessities are not wanting," Plutarch wrote. What are some of the superfluities of time, commitments, and possessions that clutter your life? How willing are you to part with these?

- Make a list of possessions you believe are necessary and important for anyone seeking to grow closer to Jesus.

Wednesday
Psalm 21:2-7
Matthew 20:1-16
(The first and the last)

At first glance, there seems to be an injustice which Jesus glosses over in today's reading. Although each group gets what it has agreed upon, it seems the partiality shown the last workers is a slight against the long-suffering group. This is a parable about the kingdom of God, however, which emphasizes that being with God will be reward enough for anyone, no matter how much the person may "deserve" admittance.

- Do you think it fair that the good thief on the cross was promised salvation by Jesus when so many of us have to work our whole lives through in faithfulness?

- "A person is not a Christian if his first concern is pay," William Barclay wrote. What should be the first concern of a Christian when considering employment?

Thursday
Psalm 40:5, 7-10
Matthew 22:1-14
(The great banquet)

Today's parable gives us another important insight into the heart of God, teaching us that God is extremely eager to share blessings with us. If we are to gain access to these blessings, we must put on the garment of faith, without which we shall never appreciate the things of God.

- What are some of the blessings you have received from the Church during the past month (*Church* meaning "people of God")? Thank God for these blessings.

- Ignatian spirituality holds that joy springs from gratitude, which springs from awareness of grace, which springs from faith. Are you a joyful person? What does this say about the way you recognize grace?

Friday
Psalm 146:5-10
Matthew 22:34-40
(The two great commandments)

Still trying to discredit Jesus, the Pharisees attempt to bait him into heresy. Jesus again proves the wiser, simplifying the Old Testament to two laws of love, both of which are dependent on and inseparable from the other.

- "The brotherhood of man is impossible unless we recognize the fatherhood of God," Taylor Caldwell wrote. Do you agree?

- "You are as close to God as you are to your neighbor" is another popular saying. Think of one way to show love to the five most important people in your life during the next week.

Saturday
Psalm 128:1-5
Matthew 23:1-12
(Humility and truth)

"Do as they say, but not as they do," Jesus counsels his disciples regarding their relationship with the scribes and Pharisees. The apparent dichotomy in this advice is necessary because Jesus respects the authority of Jewish religious leaders while disagreeing with their behavior. The principles they teach are valid, but their pride discredits them as models.

- Many theologians believe that humility means being truthful about our weaknesses *and* our strengths. How does this differ from the more traditional understanding of humility?

- How do you feel toward proud people? Is there anything you can do to become truly humble? Practice your suggestions.

- Pray for the grace to grow in humility.

Twenty-First Week in Ordinary Time

Monday
Psalm 149:1-6,9
Matthew 23:13-22
(Jesus confronts the Jewish authorities)

The goal of love is to nurture people toward growth. In today's reading we see Jesus confronting several erroneous practices of the scribes and Pharisees, challenging them to recognize their hypocrisy.

- Do you find it hard to confront a friend or relative who is doing wrong? Can you ask a person who seems to be in a rut how he or she is without being nosey?

- How would you respond to a person who says, "Christians should mind their own business unless something or someone affects them personally"?

- Pray for the grace to care enough for others to challenge them to grow.

Tuesday
Psalm 139:1
Matthew 23:23-26
(Keeping priorities straight)

Every Jew acknowledged the importance of paying tithes on crops. That the scribes and Pharisees have extended this responsibility to small plots of kitchen seasonings indicates to Jesus just how off-center they have become in their legalistic zeal. He goes on to say that commitments and responsibilities which detract from justice, mercy, and good faith will leave us empty inside.

- In what does true religion consist? Do any of your present commitments and responsibilities detract from your practice of true religion?

- With what has the cup of your soul been filled recently? Pray for the grace to be filled with love.

Wednesday
Psalm 139:7-12
Matthew 23:27-32
(Jesus denounces hypocrisy)

It is unlikely that anyone has ever confronted a group of people with more fire and sting than Jesus did the scribes and Pharisees of his day. For a Jew to come into contact with a tomb was to become unclean and, hence, unable to share in the Passover feast. By calling the scribes and Pharisees "whitewashed tombs," Jesus is saying that their hypocrisy makes them and those they contact spiritually unclean.

- How do you feel about the way Jesus confronted the Jewish authorities? Are his actions in keeping with a God of love?

- Write out a set of guidelines for confronting other people in a loving way. Make a resolution to practice these principles with someone you are concerned about during the next day.

Thursday
Psalm 90:3-4,12-14,17
Matthew 24:42-51
(Faithful servants)

We now begin to reflect on Jesus' promise to return again. "Stay awake," he counsels us, for we do not know when he will come nor when we will die. But the best reason for being faithful is not fear of punishment; we are to be faithful because it is essential to our wholeness.

- During a ball game, a saint was asked what he would do if he knew that the Lord would return to earth in fifteen minutes. "I'd finish this game of ball," he replied. Does this describe your attitude?

- "One of the most tragic things I know about human nature is that all of us tend to put off living," Dale Carnegie wrote. Resolve to make the most of this day.

Friday
Psalm 97:1-2,5-6,10-12
Matthew 25:1-13
(Preparedness pays)

Today's parable is based upon traditions that seem strange to many of us in the West. After a couple married, they went to their home and were treated like royalty by friends and relatives for several days. Late-comers were barred from this ceremony. Because no one was allowed outside at night without a light of some kind, people waiting for a nocturnal arrival of the couple needed plenty of oil if they were to gain admittance to the ceremony. In the same way, Jesus tells us, we are to be vigilant for his return.

- How do you feel when you reflect upon the fact that you will die?

- "Those who weep loudest at funerals are those who never said, 'I love you' when they had the chance," Leo Buscaglia said. How can you tell the people you care for that you love them today?

Saturday
Psalm 98:1,7-9
Matthew 25:14-30
(Parable of the talents)

Today's parable is a powerful expression of God's hopes and dreams for us. Each of us has been given a certain amount of potential. We shall be judged according to what we have done with what we have been given. Failure to develop human potential may be the gravest of all sins, for it is like a slap in the face of our Creator.

- What do you believe are your most special gifts? How are you using these to help build God's kingdom?

- How committed are you to your own personal growth? How do you feel when you are not growing as a person? How do you feel when you are experiencing a period of growth?

- Pray for the grace to love yourself enough to want to grow.

Twenty-Second Week in Ordinary Time

Monday
Psalm 96:1,3-5,11-13
Luke 4:16-30
(Jesus and the Nazarenes)

From now until Advent, we will spend time with Luke's Gospel. We begin by noting that Jesus receives mixed reviews from persons in his home town. At first they are proud of him and of his eloquence, but Jesus is not content to let them bask in the rays of this most shallow of all sources of self-worth. Worth by association counts for nothing if it is not complemented by faith and good works.

- How much self-worth do you derive from supporting certain athletic teams? From belonging to certain civic organizations? From your cultural heritage? From your denomination?

- What source of self-worth does Jesus call us to embrace? Ask for this grace.

Tuesday
Psalm 27:1,4,13-14
Luke 4:31-37
(Jesus cures a demoniac)

Outside his hometown Jesus finds people more open to his message and his healing. In today's reading we learn that he teaches with authority, quite a novelty compared to the carefully measured words of the Jewish authorities. The Holy Spirit, the source of Jesus' power and authority, silences other spirits of fragmentation, leaving the people amazed.

- Picture the scene described in today's reading from the viewpoint of a member of the crowd. Observe Jesus' encounter with the demoniac; hear the demon object to Jesus; see Jesus' face as he touches the man. Listen to the people as they say, "What is there about him?" Let your spirit be buoyed by his Spirit.

- Pray for the grace to be more self-confident.

Wednesday
Psalm 52:10-11
Luke 4:38-44
(Jesus' popularity grows)

No matter where he goes, Jesus is followed by large crowds. Many seek healing, but others probably are merely curious. Because he fears being misunderstood, Jesus forbids the evil spirits to speak of him as the Messiah. He wants to reach the people without having to work through their preconceptions.

- How does the work you do contribute to the building of God's kingdom? Do you have a sense that your work is what you have been "sent" to do? What can you do to make your daily work more enriching for yourself and others?

- Pray for the grace to find ways to love during work time.

Thursday
Psalm 98:2-6
Luke 5:1-11
(The apostles called)

We often believe that our successes are due entirely to our own efforts, hence we cultivate a self-righteous attitude that we deserve God's favor. In today's reading Jesus teaches four professional fishermen that without God's grace they cannot catch even one fish. The fishermen respond by following their Lord.

- "Work as if everything depended on you, and pray as if everything depended on God," Ignatius of Loyola advised. How close is this to your own attitude concerning work and grace?

- Spend some time with the passage "Do not be afraid. From now on you will be catching people." Allow God's desire to minister through you to pervade your entire being.

Friday
Psalm 100:1-5
Luke 5:33-39
(Jesus, the bridegroom)

Far from being rigid ascetics, Jesus and his disciples are considered quite lax when compared with other Jewish notions of spirituality. Jesus explains that he and his disciples are more interested in celebrating life than in shriveling in old traditions.

- What are some of your "old skins" that you find hardest to shed for the sake of the gospel? Pray for the grace to be willing to change these habits.

- Think of something worth celebrating today. Call it to mind several times through the day and share your joy with others.

Saturday
Psalm 54:3-4,6,8
Luke 6:1-5
(Jesus, Lord of the Sabbath)

Jewish laws were initially established to help Jewish communities live out their covenant with God in solidarity and in order. Eventually, however, these laws became like idols and the focus shifted away from God. Today's gospel describes Jesus confronting one of these examples of dehumanizing legalism.

- "God's will is the well-being of humanity," Hans Kung wrote. Do you agree with this? Why? Why not?

- In your community worship experience, on what do you focus? Is your worship Christ-oriented?

Twenty-Third Week in Ordinary Time

Monday
Psalm 62:6-7,9
Luke 6:6-11
(Healing on the Sabbath)

At times Jesus is intentionally provocative, contrary to popular notions that he was always diplomatic and mild. Today Luke describes a significant encounter between Jesus and the Jewish authorities. By healing the man with the withered hand, Jesus is responding to something which is not an emergency. On the Sabbath, according to Jewish law, intervention is permitted only in emergencies. Jesus is proving a point.

- Why do you believe Jesus chose to provoke the authorities? What did he hope to gain? What did he stand to lose?

- Have you ever found it necessary to be prophetically provocative? Are there issues requiring such a stance from you? How will you respond?

- Pray for the grace to be courageous for Christ.

Tuesday
Psalm 145:1-2,8-11
Luke 6:12-19
(Jesus chooses the Twelve)

Jesus knew that he would one day die, and he knew that he would not even begin to scratch the surface of a populated earth without the continuous ministry of his followers through the ages. That is why he called the Twelve to be his followers; that is why he still calls us to minister.

- If someone were to ask you who you are and what is important in this world, how would you answer?
- Spend some time being present to God's healing Spirit.

Wednesday
Psalm 145:2-3,10-13
Luke 6:20-26
(Blest are the poor)

Luke has simplified the list of beatitudes described in Matthew, eliminating material that his non-Jewish audience would not have properly appreciated. Nevertheless, we are left with blessings and curses which should deeply challenge us.

- Which of the beatitudes do you find most consoling? Why?
- Which of the "woes" disturb you most? Why? How does this challenge you to change?
- Pray for the grace to be willing to change for the sake of the kingdom.

Thursday
Psalm 150:1-6
Luke 6:27-38
(Love your enemies)

Jesus never denies that we will have enemies, but he does command us to recognize our enemies as fellow children of God. How to love those with whom we disagree and who oppress people is one of the most challenging tasks facing Christians today. If we do not meet this challenge, we shall be no different than animals who respond kindly to those who treat them well.

- Do you believe that Christians should do something to resist evils present in the world? Do you believe that such resistance should never be violent? Why? Why not?

- How do you feel when your efforts at kindness are unappreciated by others? Why should you persist in kindness? What will happen to *you* if you do not persist?

- Pray for the strength and wisdom to learn to resist evil in a loving spirit.

Friday
Psalm 16:1-2,5,7-8,11
Luke 6:39-42
(Do not judge)

Luke's sermon on the plain resembles Matthew's Sermon on the Mount because both include a collection of sayings and teachings of Jesus. Today's reading warns us against limiting our relationships with others by judging them harshly.

- What is the difference between forming an impression or opinion about a person and judging him or her?

- What kinds of judgments are explicit and implicit in racism, sexism, and ageism? Are you free from these shackles?

- Pray for the grace to be more open to the gifts that other people are.

Saturday
Psalm 113:1-7
Luke 6:43-49
(A firm foundation)

Human beings were created in such a fashion that we cannot live our lives immorally and spiritually without burning out. "Among all my patients in the second half of life—that is to say, over the age of thirty-five—there has not been one whose problem in the last resort was not that of finding a religious outlook on life," Carl Jung wrote. Today's reading expresses the importance of this religious foundation.

- "The figure of Christ seems to be the only one toward which human nature can tend without becoming wearied or deformed," Teilhard de Chardin wrote. Do you agree?

- What does Jesus Christ mean to you?

Twenty-Fourth Week in Ordinary Time

Monday

Psalm 28:2, 7-9
Luke 7:1-10
(Jesus heals a Gentile's servant)

"With God, all things are possible," we say at one time or another. But do we believe this? Those who do may discover, as the centurion in today's reading, that God cannot resist helping us when we are truly submissive to his will in faith and hope.

- During which period of your life was your faith strongest? How would you describe the strength of your faith at present?

- Why did the Jews plead on behalf of the centurion? What does this say about the power of love?.

- Pray for the grace to grow more deeply in faith.

Tuesday

Psalm 101:1-3,5-6
Luke 7:11-17
(Jesus raises a boy in Naim)

Jesus' actions in today's readings show us that God views the death of young people as a tragedy. In vain do we search for mysterious and hidden designs to help us understand how God can permit such tragedies, for it is God's will that we eventually eliminate them. The suffering of a woman whose child has died shall forever move the heart of Jesus.

- Do you believe in bad and good luck? Do you believe that everything that happens to people is God's will?

- Picture this scene in your imagination from the viewpoint of a disciple. Hear the wailing of the mourners as you approach the town; note the agony on the face of the mother; watch Jesus as he intervenes; experience the wonder of the moment as the boy returns to life.

Wednesday
Psalm 111:1-6
Luke 7:31-35
(You can't please everyone)

Some persons thought John the Baptist was fanatical in his asceticism; these same people probably believed that Jesus was excessive in his sensual enjoyments. Jesus is undaunted by these kinds of criticisms, however, for he has not come to please the crowds but to do his Father's will.

- Do you enjoy sensual pleasures when experienced appropriately? Do you seek out opportunities to experience and delight in good food, fresh air, sunsets, hugs and kisses?

- Pray to be open to the graces that come to us through creation.

Thursday
Psalm 111:7-10
Luke 7:36-50
(Jesus, the Pharisees, and the prostitute)

To appreciate the meaning of today's reading, we need to realize that Simon the Pharisee had denied

Jesus several hospitable gestures normally extended to guests in a Jewish home. When a woman reputed to be a sinner extends these courtesies to Jesus, he points out the relationship between her generosity and her acceptance of forgiveness.

- For what do you need to ask God's forgiveness right now? Spend some time allowing God's forgiving grace to deepen your own self-acceptance.
- Have you taken your loved ones for granted recently? If so, ask for their forgiveness and resolve to change.
- Pray for the grace to experience God's forgiveness.

Friday
Psalm 49:6-10,17-20
Luke 8:1-3
(Jesus and the women)

"It is one of the supreme achievements of Jesus that he can enable the most diverse people to live together without in the least losing their own personalities or qualities," William Barclay wrote. The group of women who followed Jesus are certainly a diverse band! But they share a common bond in their love for Jesus and their commitment to serve him out of their own meager resources.

- Do you find it difficult to establish friendships with people of opposite views? Why? Why not?
- Do you believe community is richer for including a diversity of people? Does your community include that diversity?

Saturday
Psalm 100:2-5
Luke 8:4-15
(The parable of the good seed)

Many scholars believe that the parables of Jesus are probably the best-preserved, least-manipulated accounts of his teachings. That is because stories are more easily remembered and seem to suffer less change through oral tradition than do other kinds of teachings. Today's reading gives us a glimpse of Jesus' vision of his work. He sees himself as a seed sower. Though realizing that not everyone will appreciate his words, he feels that those who do make his work worthwhile.

- What does success mean to you? Are you able to accept yourself if you do not achieve one hundred percent of what you have set out to do?

- What kinds of seeds have you sown at home recently? In your Christian community? At work?

- Spend some time inviting the Spirit to cultivate good soil in your heart.

Twenty-Fifth Week in Ordinary Time

Monday
Psalm 126:1-6
Luke 8:16-18
(Parable of the lamp)

God has blessed us with innumerable graces, bringing light to our lives. With grace comes the responsibility to extend grace to others. When we do so, we discover that special dynamism alluded to by Luke in today's reading. Those who risk and who engage themselves in life will grow in grace and experience; those who do nothing will regress.

- Make a list of the ten people to whom you are closest. How does each person enrich your life? What would your life be like without these people? Thank God for the graces they bring to you.

- "If you don't use it, you lose it" is an old biological dictum. Have you been remiss in investing any of your gifts in the service of the kingdom lately? Are you willing to let yourself regress in this area?

Tuesday
Psalm 122:1-5
Luke 8:19-21
(The Lord's family)

It is typical of Luke that he has taken the sting out of some of the more unsettling accounts about Jesus found in Mark and Matthew. Mark wrote that

Jesus' family was concerned for his sanity, but Luke simply has them paying a visit to Jesus. Today's reading shows Jesus using the occasion to affirm the primacy of our brotherhood and sisterhood under God.

- What does the communion of saints mean to you, especially that those who have died in Christ continue to work with us and intercede for us as we struggle to do God's will?

- Who is your favorite saint? How did this person reveal God? Thank God that such a person has blessed your life.

Wednesday
Tobit 13:2-4,6-8
Luke 9:1-6
(The twelve emissaries)

To insure that the Twelve apostles not be judged as having a hidden agenda and ulterior motives, Jesus sends them among the people as poor, unassuming messengers. They are to extend God's gifts of healing and teaching in return for food and shelter. If rejected, they are to move along. This model of ministry is profound in its simplicity.

- Make a list of ulterior motives that seem to hamper the efforts of Christian ministers. Do any of these motives interfere with your own efforts at spreading the Good News?

- What does the virtue of simplicity mean to you?

Thursday
Psalm 149:1-6,9
Luke 9:7-9
(Herod's paranoia)

If modern psychology has taught us anything, it is that we cannot escape the problems of life by burying our feelings. Herod the Great illustrates this truth. Guilt-ridden because he ordered the execution of John the Baptist, he begins to believe that John has risen in the person of Jesus.

- Are there crises and tragedies in your past with which you have not yet finished dealing? If so, are you willing to seek help to work your way through them?

- When was the last time you became angry at someone? How did you resolve the conflict? What did you do with your feelings of anger? (If you did nothing with them, know that conflicts with this person will probably return.)

Friday
Psalm 43:1-4
Luke 9:18-22
(Jesus and prayer)

Luke characteristically portrays Jesus as a man of prayer. Before undertaking major endeavors, Jesus is shown spending time in prayer, a model we should never ignore. In today's reading, prayer precedes Jesus' disclosure to his apostles that he is a suffering redeemer.

- Why do you pray? How has prayer helped you lately?

- Why do you believe Jesus had to "endure many sufferings, be rejected by the elders, the high priests and the scribes, and be put to death"?

- Pray for the grace to be more centered in the Spirit of Jesus.

Saturday
Jeremiah 31:10-13
Luke 9:43-45
(Passion predictions)

During the height of Jesus' ministry—when everything seems to be moving along smoothly—he warns his apostles that the tide will one day turn and he will suffer and die. Later they will appreciate his efforts to prepare them, but now his message confuses them.

- Do you believe that God wanted Jesus to be crucified?

- "Jesus died for me," we often hear Christians saying. What does this statement mean to you?

- Spend some time thanking God for the gift of his Son.

Twenty-Sixth Week in Ordinary Time

Monday
Psalm 102:16-23,29
Luke 9:46-50
(Who is the greatest?)

As Jesus' reputation has spread throughout the countryside, it is only natural that the disciples should vie for status. Christian identity has nothing to do with status or a competitive edge, however. True greatness is bestowed upon people who are open to accepting grace as a little child.

- How important is status and recognition to you? With whom do you compare yourself in evaluating your worth as a person?

- Pray for the grace to form your identity more deeply in Christ.

Tuesday
Psalm 87:1-7
Luke 9:51-56
(The journey to Jerusalem)

Chapters 9–18 in Luke differ from Mark and Matthew in that Jesus is shown journeying for the last time toward Jerusalem where he anticipates his decisive confrontation with the authorities. This literary organization is designed to help us appreciate the meaning of Jesus' life and ministry. In today's reading he proceeds through hostile territory, reprimanding James and John for their impulsive vindictiveness.

- Jesus could probably have escaped to foreign lands and lived to a ripe old age as a venerated teacher and healer. Why do you believe he chose, instead, to journey to Jerusalem where conflict was certain?

- "Don't rock the boat" is a rule implicit in bureaucracies of all kinds. How much of this spirit has pervaded your outlook? When is it appropriate to "rock the boat"? What are the risks?

Wednesday
Psalm 137:1-6
Luke 9:57-62
(A time for decision)

Following Jesus means placing his principles before all others and immediately aligning our lives with his. In today's reading we see that hesitation and excessive prudence can sometimes prevent us from making a full response to Jesus.

- Some have said that prudence should not be considered a Christian virtue. Do you agree?

- Do you believe that you are living out a full response to Jesus' invitation to follow him?

- Spend some time with the passage "Now is the time of salvation."

Thursday
Psalm 19:8-11
Luke 10:1-12
(The seventy-two emissaries)

Lacking the advantages of modern media to publicize his visitations, Jesus designates seventy-two disciples to prepare the way before him. Most noteworthy is the statement that he sends them out in pairs. Married couples might claim this passage as an affirmation of their own discipleship; single persons and celibates must recognize in it a statement which emphasizes the need for ministerial support.

- "If there is a person in your life who knows you and accepts you with all your faults, you will probably never have to worry about your mental health," Carl Jung said. Do you have such a person in your life? If not, resolve to find a spiritual director who can offer you such a grace.

- "People are lonely because they build walls instead of bridges," Joseph Newton wrote. Do you agree? Look over your coming day, anticipating times when you can build bridges.

Friday
Psalm 79:1-5,8-9
Luke 10:13-16
(Townships cursed)

Today we again return to the sobering theme of procrastinating in our response to Christ. Jesus curses Chorazin, Bethsaida, and Capernaum because they have not accepted the offer of salvation. We, too, should never take for granted Jesus' invitation to follow him. Furthermore, there are times in our lives when we are especially aware of this offer, and our responses then are crucial to our formation.

- "It only takes a moment to be loved a whole life through," John Powell said. Have you experienced such peak moments in your life? Did you ever withdraw from the promise of such a moment?

Pray for the grace to recognize and accept these invitations when they come.

- Spend some time with the verse "He who hears you, hears me." What does this say to you about the importance of your example to others?

Saturday
Psalm 69:33-37
Luke 10:17-24
(The joy of Jesus)

Is there more to life than pleasurable experiences or happiness? Yes, there is the joy of the Holy Spirit, as today's reading shows us. While pleasure comes with sensual gratification and is short-lived, and happiness comes from striving to realize personal goals, joy is deeper, rooted in an awareness of the great things God has done for us.

- What kind of person do you think you would be if you were not a Christian? Spend some time considering the many ways your Christian faith has helped make you a better person.

- Pray with Jesus: "I offer you grateful praise, O Father, Lord of heaven and earth." Repeat this prayer of praise again and again as your heart wells up with joy.

Twenty-Seventh Week in Ordinary Time

Monday
Jonah 2:2-5,8
Luke 10:25-37
(Parable of the Good Samaritan)

"And who is my neighbor?" the lawyer asks Jesus in earnest. Many rabbis interpreted God's commandment to love one's neighbor as a summons to love only Jews. Jesus counters this elitism by posing a story about a Samaritan who is a model of the true neighbor, closer to God's heart than the Jewish priest who hurries along, ignoring the man on the side of the road. Since Samaritans were despised by the Jews, Jesus' parable must have stung his listeners.

- Who are the "people in the bushes" ignored in today's world? How do you respond to their needs?

- "Jesus was the only teacher tall enough to see over the fences that divide the human race into compartments," Frank Crane wrote. Pray for the grace to be able to see people as Christ sees them.

Tuesday
Psalm 130:1-4,7-8
Luke 10:38-42
(Mary and Martha)

We are constantly required to make decisions; at any moment we can direct our attention to many concerns. In the story of Mary and Martha, Jesus affirms Mary because she has chosen wisely in setting her priorities. The dishes can be done later; Martha's fretting over the "details of hospitality" are less important than being present to the Son of God.

- How do you make value decisions concerning the focus of your attention during each day? What happens to your attention when you do not consciously direct it toward a specific matter, either external or internal?

- "God does not want our presents; he wants our presence" is an old aphorism. Spend some time simply being present to the Lord, basking in the rays of his love.

Wednesday
Psalm 86:3-6,9-10
Luke 11:1-4
(The Lord's Prayer)

Luke's version of the prayer of Jesus is shorter than Matthew's, characteristic of his commitment to simplify the words of Jesus. We are nevertheless left with the essentials emphasized in Matthew's version: praise, kingdom, dependence, forgiveness, and perseverance.

- Which phrase from the Lord's Prayer do you find easiest to pray? Which is most difficult? Why?

- What kind of God does Jesus reveal through this prayer?

Thursday
Psalm 1:1-4,6
Luke 11:5-13
(The value of persistence)

Jesus often taught about God by using analogies in human behavior. One of his most frequent themes is that God is at least as good as good human beings. God is therefore approachable, interested, and willing to help us if we take the trouble to address him.

- "The poor man is not he who is without a cent, but he who is without a dream," Harry Kemp wrote. What are some of your dreams for the future? How do you keep these dreams alive?

- What are you doing to keep yourself growing and learning about the spiritual life?

- Pray for the grace to dream "the impossible dream."

Friday
Psalm 9:2-3,6,8-9,16
Luke 11:15-26
(Jesus and Beelzebul)

To discredit Jesus' ministry, some people begin accusing him of doing the work of Satan. Jesus not only counters the contradictions apparent in such accusations but also states that people who are not with him are working against him. There is really no middle ground in life upon which a person may claim neutrality toward God.

- Looking back over the events of the past several days, do you see yourself moving toward or away from God? Explain.

- What kind of "unclean spirit" has been troubling you lately? How can you displace it with love? Make a plan and pray for the grace to carry out your resolve.

Saturday
Psalm 97:1-2,5-6,11-12
Luke 11:27-28
(True blessings)

Again we hear a message ringing through the gospels: Knowing Jesus and simply being related to him in a superficial way counts for nothing. "Even the devils believe in God," James wrote, and the devils recognized Jesus as the Messiah. If we are to really grow in Christ, we must act on God's word.

- Which Christian values do you have the most trouble understanding? Resolve to speak to someone who can help you to comprehend what God is calling you to in this area.

- Spend some time with the verse "Blest are [you] who hear the word of God and observe it."

Twenty-Eighth Week in Ordinary Time

Monday
Psalm 98:1-4
Luke 11:29-32
(Seekers of grace)

Many people live in countries where the freedom to worship is diminished or prohibited by oppressive governments. The least we who live in free countries can do is to take advantage of the many opportunities for growth present in our society. Jesus commended the Queen of Sheba and the Ninevites for making the most of their opportunities to grow in grace; he affirms us if we do likewise.

- When was the last time you made a retreat or day of recollection? Look into the possibility of scheduling one soon.

- What are some signs of God's presence that you have observed recently? Thank God for these reassurances of his love for you.

Tuesday
Psalm 19:2-5
Luke 11:37-41
(Confrontation at a Pharisee's home)

Some of the Pharisees must have been friendly toward Jesus' cause. Indeed, Paul often found them to be more sympathetic to the gospel than were the scribes or the Sadducees. When Jesus chooses to ignore certain rituals of cleanliness in a Pharisee's home, he is being deliberately provocative. This incident gives him an opportunity to confront the legalism of his host, calling the Pharisee to re-examine his priorities.

- Many people believe that Jesus' criticism of the Pharisee in today's reading can be applied to society today. What do you think?

- Why would almsgiving help transform the heart of the Pharisees? How does giving of your time and talent in the service of others transform you?

Wednesday
Psalm 62:2-3,6-7,9
Luke 11:42-46
("Woe to you...")

If we saw a friend backing toward the edge of a cliff, we would certainly yell out a warning. Similarly, Jesus feels compelled to warn the scribes and Pharisees that some of their beliefs and practices are hurting themselves and others.

- "He has the right to criticize who has the heart to help," Abraham Lincoln wrote. Does this criterion apply to Jesus?

- Of what practices in the Church are you most critical? What are you doing to help improve these situations?

Thursday
Psalm 130:1-6
Luke 11:47-54
(More woes)

How easy it is to honor a holy person after they've died, but how difficult to tolerate the words and deeds of a living saint. When Jesus confronts the scribes and Pharisees for precisely this hypocrisy, he arouses only their animosity. They are too proud to change.

- Of what practices in our society are you most critical? What are you doing to counter these practices?

- Do you avoid arguments when it is obvious that the others are not open to changing? Why? Why not?

Friday
Psalm 32:1-2,5,11
Luke 12:1-7
(Fear God alone)

People who are afraid are not free, Jesus tells us in today's reading. "Perfect love casts out all fear" John wrote in his epistle. If we could eliminate from our lives the fear of death and the fear of harsh judgments from others, we would be truly free. If we really believe that God loves us unconditionally, this fear will leave us.

- When do you most often experience fear and anxiety? How do you usually handle these feelings? How can you change your thinking concerning these occasions to diminish fear? Write out suggestions for yourself.

- Spend some time with the verse "Do not be afraid. You are worth more than many sparrows."

Saturday
Psalm 105:6-9,42-43
Luke 12:8-12
(The unforgivable sin)

It takes faith and courage to publicly affirm Jesus as lord and savior of our lives and of the world. To deny that God can change a person, however, is to sin against the Holy Spirit, for such a denial makes one incapable of repenting and taking hold of the only source of grace. How terrible for us when we have lost such faith in God!

- Have you ever given up on yourself and your ability to cope with life? If so, spend a few moments reflecting on how far you have come since then.

- How have you acknowledged the Son of Man while at work recently? At home? How will you acknowledge him before people today?

- Pray for the grace to be true to your faith in times of crisis.

Twenty-Ninth Week in Ordinary Time

Monday
Psalm 100:2-5
Luke 12:13-21
(On materialism)

We should never make the mistake of assuming that Christianity is completely unconcerned with material goods. How cruel it would be for a Christian to chide a hungry or unemployed person because he or she is not concerned about spiritual matters! Jesus recognizes our human need for basic material goods but warns us not to rely on these transient riches for security.

- Spend some time with the verse "Though one may be rich, one's life does not consist of possessions." What or who can guarantee life?

- Is it possible for a person to be a follower of Jesus and be wealthy? Why? Why not?

Tuesday
Psalm 40:7-10,17
Luke 12:35-38
(Stay awake)

How wonderful it is to love someone and to be aware that this person is watching your every move in utter delight! This is exactly how God regards us. As we grow in our love of God, we shall become more aware and eager to be completely united with him.

- Many philosophers have said that consciousness

is what makes us different from animals. Do you agree?

- Today to spend a few moments contemplating the wonder of a God who loves you and delights in you. Let this wonder refresh you.

Wednesday
Psalm 124:1-8
Luke 12:39-48
(Honesty and fidelity)

The world is a much better place because of the Judeo-Christian doctrine of an eventual call to judgment. But fear of punishment is, at best, only a minimal reason to remain faithful to God. Fidelity to Christ's values is strongest in people who recognize in these principles a way to live life to the fullest. Those who never achieve this understanding will not be judged as harshly as will those who do know the truth but choose selfishness anyway.

- What are some of the reasons why you faithfully follow Jesus?

- "When you know the right thing to do but do not do it, you sin," James wrote. Spend some time reflecting on how lately you have fallen short of the goodness to which Jesus calls you. Ask God for forgiveness.

Thursday
Psalm 1:1-4,6
Luke 12:49-53
(The fire of Christ)

"Peace at any price" is not a slogan a Christian should adopt as a guiding principle. Although it is true that Jesus is often called the Prince of Peace, we must realize that the peace he brings cannot exist outside of the context of truth and love. Some people will not recognize truth, others will reject love; therefore, Christians ought to expect persecutions.

- "If you want peace, work for justice" is a slogan adopted by the U.S. Catholic bishops. Do you agree with this slogan? Why? Why not?

- Has your Christian faith brought divisions in your family? If so, what can you do to remain related to family members without compromising your beliefs?

Friday
Psalm 119:66, 68, 76-77, 93-94
Luke 12:54-59
(The signs of the times)

We have become quite adept at understanding God's creation and of prospering from it. We have placed people on the moon and learned the secrets of the atom. We have a technology which promises wonders only dreamed of by science fiction writers in the past. Yet we have achieved only minimal ethical and spiritual progress through the ages. In today's reading Jesus tells us that we ought to apply our intelligence to the things of God as much as to creation and materialism.

- "People do not change, only culture" is a familiar maxim. Do you agree with this? Why? Why not?

- What are some of the signs of the times today to which we ought to pay more attention? What are you doing to take a stand?

Saturday
Psalm 24:1-6
Luke 13:1-9
(The patience of Christ)

In today's reading Jesus teaches us a lesson that goes against many popular notions. Galileans murdered by Pilate and people killed by a falling tower are simply victims of circumstances, he tells us. Never let us suppose that tragedy is a judgment of God against someone. Instead, let us be compassionate toward the unfortunate, for their fate is not necessarily deserved.

- Do you believe that God causes human suffering? What can we learn from suffering if we persevere in faith and love?

- How do you feel toward those less fortunate than yourself? What do you do with your feelings of self-righteousness?

- Pray for the grace to be more accepting of yourself and others.

Thirtieth Week in Ordinary Time

Monday
Psalm 68:2,4,6-7,20-21
Luke 13:10-17
(Jesus heals on the Sabbath)

Today's reading teaches us an important lesson. Because Jesus heals a woman on the Sabbath, he provokes the wrath of the chief of the synagogue. He responds to this indignation by pointing out that people are more important than animals and laws. Christianity alone is the religion of the individual.

- Do you believe that the Spirit of Jesus heals today? If you do, then how is God effecting healing through you?

- Have you neglected contacting certain friends and family members lately? Resolve to communicate during the coming week with at least two with whom you have lost touch.

Tuesday
Psalm 126:1-5
Luke 13:18-21
(Growth of the kingdom)

Is history going somewhere? This is a very important question to which various religions give different replies. Eastern religions like Buddhism and Hinduism espouse a circular view of history, with little or no real progress being made in human spiritual growth. Religions springing from the Judeo-

Christian tradition propose a linear view of history, with progress toward the full realization of God's kingdom growing slowly but surely through the years—as a mustard seed grows into a shrub and yeast grows in a batch of dough.

- Do you believe that individuals can change for the better through the years? Do you believe that societies can change for the better? Why? Why not?

- Spend some time being present to God, asking that the Holy Spirit leaven your own spirit unto love.

Wednesday
Psalm 13:4-6
Luke 13:22-30
(The narrow gate)

If we have not already heard this message enough, we need to listen again: Salvation does not come because we know about Jesus. In today's reading we hear Jesus promising to reject people who claim familiarity with him but who do nothing to help their needy neighbors. The narrow road he invites us to walk is the difficult path of love.

- Do you believe that some people will go to hell, that they will be separated from God for all eternity? Why? Why not?

- List some of the key events of your past two days. How would you describe the spiritual road that threads through these events?

- Pray for the grace to embrace difficult times in a spirit of perseverance.

Thursday
Psalm 109:21-22,26-27,30-31
Luke 13:31-35
(Jesus and Herod)

Though Herod was king of Galilee, he was little more than a puppet of Rome. Still feeling guilty over his murder of John the Baptist, he has decided to kill Jesus who reminds him of John. But friendly Pharisees alert Jesus to the danger. Jesus has his heart set on Jerusalem, however, and will not be denied his destiny.

- What kind of man calls a king a fox? Why was Jesus unafraid of Herod?

- What are some of the key secular issues of the day? How are you taking a stand?

Friday
Psalm 147:12-15,19-20
Luke 14:1-6
(Healing again on the Sabbath)

Although Luke does not say it explicitly, one can sense that the reason the Pharisee has invited Jesus to his home is to keep an eye on him and to get information that can be used to discredit Jesus. Jesus again challenges the Pharisees to leave their legalism behind and embrace the law of love.

- What are some of the idols of the day which deny the value of the individual? How are you taking a stand to work through these influences?

- Pray for the grace to see people as more important than anything else.

Saturday
Psalm 94:12-15,17-18
Luke 14:1,7-11
(The first and the last)

Still under surveillance, Jesus refuses to assume a defensive posture toward the Pharisees. Social status has been a primary hindrance to spiritual growth for many of them, so he finds a teachable moment during a dinner party to invite them to become truly humble.

- Do you know a friend or family member who is following the idol of social status? How can you confront this person in a manner which shows your love and concern for his or her spiritual growth?

- Do you discipline your own desire to impress others and feed your ego? Make a plan to stave off this weakness when it occurs.

Thirty-First Week in Ordinary Time

Monday
Psalm 69:30-31,33-34,36-37
Luke 14:12-14
(Agape love)

To help the Pharisees work through their preoccupation over status and discover *agape*, the love which God shows for us, Jesus suggests they reach out to those who cannot possibly repay them. If we, too, were to heed Jesus' advice, we would discover an opportunity to love as God loves.

- Have you ever loved or given with no expectation of return? If so, get in touch with the feelings you experienced. If not, think of a way to give today without expecting something in return.

- Why do you believe God loves you? Pray for the grace to view other people likewise.

Tuesday
Psalm 131:1-3
Luke 14:15-24
(Good excuses for the damned)

God created because God is love, and love seeks to share its joy with others. God chose a people and attempted to prepare them to appreciate the gifts they would receive—especially the gift of the Son—but they were too busy with their own agenda. Therefore, Jesus tells us in today's reading, the invitation shall now be extended to anyone who wants to share the Lord's joy.

- "Life is what happens to us while we're making other plans," Ann Landers wrote. What do you think she meant by this?

- What are some of the excuses you use to keep yourself distanced from the needs of others? How many of these are legitimate?

Wednesday
Psalm 112:1-2,4-5,9
Luke 14:25-33
(Pick up your cross)

The cross is an intensely powerful Christian symbol because it describes so well the quality of love which God expects of us. Christianity alone has been able to extract meaning from human suffering, for our God has suffered with us. Those who decide to follow Jesus can expect struggles and hardships, but perseverance will bring deeper love and new life.

- What battle plan have you developed for your life? What obstacles might frustrate these plans? Where does the cross enter?

- Pray for the grace to remain faithful to Jesus when inconveniences confront you.

Thursday
Psalm 27:1,4,13-14
Luke 15:1-10
(Two parables of mercy)

God's will may sometimes be difficult to discern, but we may always be certain God desires that people come to know and love the One who sent Jesus. We should, therefore, pray for those who have fallen away and make every effort to help souls turn toward Jesus who leads us to God. When we do so, we can expect to share in the joy of the angels.

- Do you feel it is your business to try to influence other people to embrace Jesus? Why? Why not?

- If a person is kind and virtuous but does not believe in Jesus, should a Christian try to influence him or her to become a believer?

- Pray that those who reach out to others may persevere in love.

Friday
Psalm 98:1-4
Luke 16:1-8
(The clever manager)

At first glance, this appears to be a parable of forgiveness, but it is much more. When Jesus commends the manager for his cleverness in assuring his future, he also chides his followers for their lack of initiative in the things of God. What if we were to give as much time and effort to building the kingdom of God as we do to securing a living and advancing ourselves professionally? What would the world be like?

- Divide a sheet of paper into three columns. In the first column, list activities in which you are regularly engaged (employment, sleep, recreation, for example). In the second column, write the amount of time you spend each week on each activity. In the third column, list the reasons why you engage in each activity. Study this list awhile, praying for wisdom to help you reorganize your life, if necessary.

Saturday
Psalm 145:2-5,10-11
Luke 16:9-15
(On God and money)

This collection of sayings stresses the importance of being honest with ourselves concerning our attachments to wealth. Significantly, these verses seem to say that our spiritual charity should be balanced by our generosity with material goods. The world may consider this a laughable notion, but God's priorities are often different from those of the world.

- Look over your reflection from yesterday and determine what you perceive are the top three priorities in your life (consider time and rationale, for example). On another sheet of paper, enter the same three column headings and then write in the activities, time commitments, and motives you eventually want to fill your life. How different is your second life sketch from the first? Why?

- Resolve to do something today to begin to bring your life more in line with where you want to go.

Thirty-Second Week in Ordinary Time

Monday
Psalm 139:1-10
Luke 17:1-6
(The importance of good example)

Because God reveals himself to us through human behavior, those of us committed to following Jesus Christ should be especially careful not to scandalize the innocent and the ignorant. It is, therefore, our duty to confront one another when we veer away from a life of love.

- "He who cannot forgive breaks the bridge over which he himself must pass," George Herbert wrote. How does withholding forgiveness hurt you?

- Is there a friend or loved one whose alcohol and/or drug use concerns you? If you are not sure how to confront this person, call a substance abuse counselor for help.

Tuesday
Psalm 34:2-3,16-19
Luke 17:7-10
(Christian duty)

There are many times when we feel that our ministries of service should entitle us to extraordinary recognition. This temptation to impress others with our goodness should be countered by an admission that what we have done is not extraordinary but rather our duty.

- What are some reasons why you fear reaching out? Resolve to work through at least one of these blocks to relationship.

- What are some of the ways you can affirm your loved ones for their love "duties" which you have recently taken for granted?

Wednesday
Psalm 82:3-4,6-7
Luke 17:11-19
(The attitude of gratitude)

Life is such an incredible phenomenon! It is possible that our planet alone out of billions of galaxies and stars is hospitable to living organisms. How sad it is that we do not properly appreciate the miracle that we are! Gratitude brought the Samaritan leper far more than health; it brought him salvation.

- Do you believe it is a sin to take your life and creation for granted?

- Spend time thanking God for the gift of your life, your body and its functioning parts, your health, your energy.

Thursday
Psalm 119:89-91,130,135,175
Luke 17:20-25
(The kingdom among us)

An erroneous translation in the past said that "The kingdom of God is within you." The more correct translation is "The kingdom of God is among you." The implication of the new translation is that God's Spirit is most active in our relationships with one another.

- Where do you look for God? How can you tell when you are experiencing God?

- Spend some time with the passage "The reign of God is already in your midst." Pray for the grace to recognize God's presence throughout the day.

Friday
Psalm 19:2-5
Luke 17:26-37
(The end times)

The life, death, and resurrection of Jesus is a paradigm for the direction which history is to take. "He didn't teach us how to swim only to let us drown," the Imperials sing. This does not mean Christians will be spared the experience of catastrophe, however. Even Jesus had to pick up his own cross and face the powers of evil in this world.

- Do you believe God will allow nuclear warfare to occur? Why? Why not?

- Do you, as Paul did nineteen hundred years ago, entertain the hope that Jesus will return before you die? Is this a way to cope with your fear of death?

Saturday
Psalm 105:2-3,36-37,42-43
Luke 18:1-8
(Persist in prayer)

"God is at least as good as a corrupt judge who, after all, gave in to the requests of a persistent widow," Jesus tells us in today's parable. It is when the going gets tough that our degree of faith will show itself. If our faith is weak, we shall be over-whelmed by life's difficulties; if our faith is strong, we shall conquer the world.

- Do you find it difficult to pray when anxieties and suffering wear you down? How do you feel when you try to cope on your own?

- Ask God to give you the grace to work through a problem with which you've struggled recently. Believe that grace is yours and resolve to work through this difficulty in a spirit of honesty and love.

Thirty-Third Week in Ordinary Time

Monday
Psalm 119:53,61,134,150,155,158
Luke 18:35-43
(The blind see)

Today we reflect on another example of the value of persistence. The blind man will not be denied his opportunity to meet Jesus and request healing from him. Jesus rewards his faith by granting his request.

- Jesus must have known what the blind man wanted, so why did he ask, "What do you want me to do for you?"

- Do you find it difficult to articulate your needs to others? If so, how are they to know how you need them to love you?

Tuesday
Psalm 3:2-8
Luke 19:1-10
(Jesus and Zacchaeus)

Tax collectors were men designated by Rome to extract from the Jews money owed Rome for services rendered by the government. They were despised by the Jews; many Jews resented being governed by Rome, and tax collectors often extorted money for their own enrichment. Zacchaeus, the chief tax collector, must have been the focal point of much hatred, but this does not stop him from seeking out Jesus and subsequently reforming his life.

- Would you be willing to climb a tree to see Jesus? Do you empathize with Zacchaeus' desire to be with Jesus?

- Resolve to invite to dinner someone with whom you have had little contact recently.

- Pray to desire a deeper relationship with Jesus.

Wednesday
Psalm 17:1,5-6,8,15
Luke 19:11-28
(Parable of the pounds)

Jesus may have based this story on an actual historical occurrence. When Herod the Great died, one of his sons, Archelaus, went to Rome to plead for his inheritance. A delegation of Jews dissuaded the emperor from appointing him king, though his inheritance was granted. Jesus builds this incident into a lesson about the wise use of our talents.

- "So, because you are lukewarm, neither hot nor cold, I will spit you out of my mouth," the risen Christ said to the Church in Laodicea (Revelation 3:16). What does this passage say to you?

- Have you been developing your talents and sharing yourself in challenging ways lately? How?

Thursday
Psalm 50:1-2,5-6,14-15
Luke 19:41-44
(Jesus weeps over Jerusalem)

God wants so very much for us, and we often settle for so very little! This is what Jesus laments as he stands outside the gates of Jerusalem, longing to share with the people of the city his many graces. He knows he will be rejected, however, so he weeps for the suffering this will bring to his people.

- What are some reasons why we settle for less than what God wants to give us? With which of these blocks to growth have you recently struggled?

- Are you satisfied with the promises made and goods delivered by proponents of the great American dream? Why? Why not?

- Pray for the grace to hunger for the things of God.

Friday
1 Chronicles 29:10-12
Luke 19:45-48
(Cleansing the Temple)

To appreciate the zeal which moved Jesus to expel the traders in the Temple, we must realize that the moneychangers and sellers of animals who had set up booths were victimizing the poor, offering services at elevated prices. This defilement of the people of God in the name of his house angered Jesus.

- How do you feel about your tax dollars supporting oppressive military regimes throughout the world?

- How do you feel about your lord marching into the midst of his enemies and confronting them?
- Pray for the grace to be courageous in your beliefs.

Saturday
Psalm 9:2-4,6,16,19
Luke 20:27-40
(Confronting the Sadducees)

Because the conservative Sadduccees did not believe in life after death, their notions of justice applied only to this life. When they present their hypothetical case to Jesus to test him, Jesus promises that children of the Resurrection shall live with God forever. This promise should bring joy to us today.

- Do you ever fantasize about what heaven might be like? If a non-believer were to ask you why anyone should hope for heaven, what answer would you give?
- "I consider that the sufferings of this present time are as nothing compared with the glory to be revealed for us," Paul wrote (Romans 8:18). Spend some time letting this hope buoy your spirit.

Thirty-Fourth Week in Ordinary Time

Monday
Daniel 3:52-56
Luke 21:1-4
(True giving)

During this last week of the Church's liturgical year, we will consider some of the most important of all Christian truths. Today's short reading teaches us that when we give of our excess we have given very little of ourselves. Real giving involves risk— not only of financial resources, but of mental and spiritual resources also.

- "The door into the kingdom of God opens from the inside out" is a popular saying. "You may have an abundance for every good work," Paul added (2 Corinthians 9:7). How do you understand these adages? Have you experienced these truths working in your life recently? How can you work them today?

- Pray for the grace to recognize opportunities to give of yourself.

Tuesday
Daniel 3:57-61
Luke 21:5-11
(The destruction of the Temple)

The Temple which existed in Jerusalem at the time of Jesus had taken decades to rebuild. Many believe it rivaled the Temple built by Solomon in beauty and size. It was destroyed, however, by Vespasius' troops as they decisively repressed Jewish insurrections in A.D. 70. In today's reading Jesus warns us that the coming of God's kingdom will be accompanied by wars, destruction, and suffering.

- Some philosophers maintain that either God can prevent evil but chooses not to, or he cannot prevent evil even though he might want to do so. What is your response to this statement?

- We live today in a world of economic insecurity and political unrest where peace depends on nuclear might. How does the peace of Jesus sustain you in the midst of these situations?

Wednesday
Daniel 3:62-67
Luke 21:12-19
(Persevere through persecutions)

Because Christians recognize that the status quo is never a full manifestation of the kingdom of God, we shall be persecuted by the idolaters of the status quo. Perseverance in love and truth shall win us a place in eternity, however, for our Lord has gone before us.

- Do you believe that heroism is dead? What are some "ordinary" examples of heroism with which you are familiar? Why have these people persevered in such noble ways?

- What are examples of heroic perseverance from your own life? How did you grow because of these experiences?

Thursday
Daniel 3:68-74
Luke 21:20-28
(The Second Coming)

The Church has always believed that her risen Lord would return. Just how, when, and where this will occur we do not know, despite the insistence of fundamentalist exegetes to the contrary. Jesus' teachings concerning his return come to us couched in the words of apocalyptic literature which is highly symbolic and difficult to understand. It is enough for us to believe that history will not terminate in some catastrophic dead end; Christ shall one day be "all in all."

- What does the Second Coming mean to you?
- Do you believe you will be faced with the prospect of living through personal and/or national catastrophe before you die? If so, how do you propose to remain hopeful when those times come?

Friday
Daniel 3:75-81
Luke 21:29-33
(Parable of the fig tree)

Just as a fig tree shows signs when it is going to flower and bear fruit, so do ordinary circumstances give hints at what is to come. This does not mean that we ought to leave the future to itself, withdrawing from the world in fatalistic pessimism, however. Nothing could be farther from the Spirit of Jesus Christ.

- "Never put off something that can and should be done today" is a wise saying. Resolve to make a fresh start in whatever endeavors you have been avoiding recently.

- Spend some time with the passage "Heaven and earth will pass away, but my words will not pass." Invite the Holy Spirit to deepen your rootedness in God's love.

Saturday
Daniel 3:82-87
Luke 21:34-36
(Be watchful)

Jesus came that we might know God and that the power of sin in this world might be broken. His Spirit enables us to stand before God in peace and security, knowing that the kingdom which Jesus came to build shall eventually displace the kingdom of the world. That this vision might be realized, God invites us to strive constantly to grow in love, resisting indulgence and worldly cares. This struggle is a lifelong process.

- "Show me a thoroughly satisfied man, and I will show you a failure," Thomas Edison wrote. What did he mean by this?

- "Christianity is not a religion of ends, but one of means," another great thinker wrote. Do you believe that crooked means can ever produce straight ends? Why? Why not?

- Spend some time thanking God for the graces that have come to you through the Church's liturgical ministry.

About the Author

Philip St. Romain is the author of numerous books on spirituality and prayer and the coauthor of *Living Together, Loving Together: A Spiritual Guide to Marriage* with his wife, Lisa. He writes the popular "The Counselor's Mailbox" column for *Liguorian*, a monthly magazine, and has contributed articles to other publications.

He earned his B.S. and M.S. degrees from the University of Southwestern Louisiana. A certified substance abuse counselor, he worked in that field for ten years before becoming associate director of the Spiritual Life Center in the Diocese of Wichita (KS). He also serves as a spiritual director and a retreat director.

When he is not writing or working, he enjoys gardening and golfing. He is married to author Lisa Bellecci-st.romain; they live with their three children in Wichita, Kansas.